Between Two Gardens

Other books by James B. Nelson

The Responsible Christian
Moral Nexus: Ethics of Christian Identity and Community
Human Medicine: Ethical Perspectives on New Medical Issues
Rediscovering the Person in Medical Care
Embodiment: An Approach to Sexuality and Christian Theology

Between Two Gardens

Reflections
on Sexuality and
Religious Experience

by

JAMES B. NELSON

The Pilgrim Press
New York

Fourth printing, 1988

Library of Congress Cataloging in Publication Data

Nelson, James Bruce.
  Between two gardens.

  Includes bibliographical references.
  1. Sex—Religious aspects—Christianity.   I. Title.
BT708.N43   1983   241'.66   83-11119
ISBN 0-8298-0681-4

The Pilgrim Press, 132 West 31 Street, New York, NY 10001

To several special friends,
whose encouragement
has meant much to me

CONTENTS

PREFACE

*F*or the greater share of the Christian era we have asked essentially a one-directional question concerning religion and sexuality: what does the faith (the Bible, the tradition, current theological opinion, etc.) say about our human sexuality, what it means, and how we ought to express it? This is an important question that needs constantly to be asked and wrestled with. But there is a second question, equally important: what does our experience as human sexual beings have to say about the way we do theology, read the scriptures, interpret the tradition, and attempt to live out the meanings of the gospel?

I believe there is a genuine need for *sexual theology*. This is more than simply a theology about sexuality. It is more than sexual ethics. In its method a sexual theology takes some cues from the various liberation theologies. Such theologies—coming from feminists, third-world Christians, blacks, gays, and lesbians—attempt to take seriously the implications of the faith for each group's own situation. But just as significantly, these theologies take seriously the implications of their experiences as oppressed groups for understanding the gospel.

I began using the term sexual theology several years ago in *Embodiment: An Approach to Sexuality and Christian Theology*. Since that time I have become increasingly convinced that the concept is needed and appropriate. Conversations with a wide spectrum of persons and groups have impressed me even more than before with the significance of human sexuality for the life of faith, and with the importance of the journey to integrate the two, both theologically and experientially.

A number of the chapters in this book were originally written for presentation elsewhere, both as lectures and as articles. I have revised them for inclusion here. Even with revision, the tone and style of the chapters vary. Some are more personal and confessional, some more formal and analytical. Perhaps both approaches have their usefulness in exploring some of the dimensions of a sexual theology for our time.

I wish to express my thanks to United Theological Seminary of the Twin Cities for encouraging me to write this book and for providing secretarial assistance. Barbara J. Nelson deserves special mention.

It is a genuine pleasure to acknowledge gratitude to a number of audiences and to the gracious people who hosted me for the original presentations of some of this material: Queen's Theological College, Kingston, Ontario (The Chancellor's Lectures); Kirkridge Retreat Center, Bangor, Pennsylvania (The Pilgrimage of Faith); The Associated Church Press (Annual Convention); St. Olaf College (Spring Symposium); The Center for Judaic Studies, University of Denver (Symposium on Sexuality in the Jewish and Christian Traditions); The American Lutheran Church and Pacific Lutheran Theological Seminary (Conference on Singles and the Church); United Church Board for Homeland Ministries (Conference on Religious Piety and Political Reaction); Evangelical Hospital Association, Chicago (Seventy-fifth Anniversary Celebration); Luther Northwestern Seminary (Convocation); and the Presbyterian Church in Canada (National Consultation on the Theology of Sexuality). I also want to record with special pleasure thanks to my class in Incarnation and Ethics, United Theological Seminary of the Twin Cities, for critical dialogue about some of these issues, especially those in chapter 2.

Further, I acknowledge with appreciation the permission of the following publishers for allowing me to use in this volume adapted and revised versions of materials that originally appeared in their publications: *Studies in Formative Spirituality*, Duquesne University (chapter 1); *Marriage & Family Review* (chapter 4); University of Denver (chapter 5); "Homosexuality & Psychotherapy," a special issue of the *Journal of Homosexuality* (vol. 7, no. 2/3), The Haworth Press, Inc., 1982 (chapter 7); *Theological Markings*, United Theological Seminary (chapter 8); *New Conversations* (Fall 1981), United Church Board for Homeland Ministries (chapter 9); *The Bulletin* and *The Challenge* (July 1982), Evangelical Hospital Association (chapter 11). Chapter 10 is a revision of "Abortion: Protestant Perspectives" by James B. Nelson. Reprinted with permission of The Free Press, a Division of Macmillan Publishing Co., Inc., and the Kennedy Institute of Ethics, Georgetown University. From *Encyclopedia of Bioethics*, Warren T. Reich, Editor-in-Chief, Volume 1, pages 13–17. Copyright © 1978 by Georgetown University, Washington, DC.

Perhaps we human beings only dimly understand the connections between incarnation and sexuality. To grapple with them as best we can is the task of the kind of thinking that might emerge from the whole body-self, drawing on both our cognitive and our affective capacities. Yet our thinking has its limits. Our hunger for communication and communion outruns our capacity to understand. Thus the Word becoming flesh will remain in some large measure mystery and unarticulated experience. But even when we do not understand, we might experience that to which D.H. Lawrence referred in saying, "We don't exist unless we are deeply and sensually in touch with that which can be touched but not known."[1]

Between Two Gardens

Between Two Gardens: Reflections on Spirituality and Sexuality

The experience occurred during a midnight eucharistic service on Christmas Eve several years ago. I was on a sabbatical leave in Cambridge, England. My wife and I and several friends, having celebrated the earlier part of the evening with good food and conversation, were at the late evening service at King's College Chapel. As Gothic buildings go, surely that is one of the most glorious. And it is gloriously sexual. Its thrusting phallic towers frame those labial doors leading to the interior womb. There is serenity within, but with it a marked sensuousness. During the day soft light filters through the elegant stained glass, and during evening services the candles cast their glow on dark wood mellowed by centuries of worshipers. And, of course, King's Chapel is the home of some of the finest choral and organ music to be heard anywhere.

Then there is the Rubens painting. Mounted above the altar is Peter Paul Rubens' *Adoration of the Magi*. While he had never been a favorite artist of mine (somehow his work seemed a bit too voluptuous), I had studied that painting from time to time in previous visits to the chapel and found myself increasingly attracted to it. At the center are Mary and the babe. Surrounding them are Joseph, the magi, and their companions. Hovering above are two cherubic angels. The colors are warm, even erotic: reds, golds, blues. But most striking is the manner in which every other figure in the painting is reaching out toward the infant Christ. Reaching in wonder, desire, longing. Reaching toward fulfillment.

As I knelt at the altar rail to receive the sacrament, I found myself unusually moved by wonder, desire, and longing. More surprising than the intensity of the emotions themselves were the bodily sensations. I was feeling unmistakable sexual arousal. My entire body-self was longing for the divine. "The Desire of Nations" had become a compelling personal desire. Eros and agape seemed merged.

I have since reflected on that experience from time to time. That it was an unusual occurrence is undoubted proof of my own continuing spiritual fragmentation. But the fact that in that moment (and on some other occasions less dramatically) I *knew* that the Christian spiritual life is meant to involve the totality of the self—yes, the sexual self—provides a continuing promise and hope.

Paul Ricoeur has observed three major stages in the evolution of Western understandings of sexuality in relation to religion.[1] The earliest stage, he notes, identified two realms. Sexuality was incorporated into the believer's total understanding of reality through patterns of myth, ritual, and symbol. When the great religions arose during the second stage there came a separation. Now the sacred was experienced as transcendent, untouchable, separate—heavenly and not earthly. The meanings of sexuality were demythologized and limited to a small part of the total order, essentially that of procreation within the institution of marriage. The power of sexuality was to be restrained by discipline, and when sexual expression threatened to break out of the prescribed order its power was feared and condemned.

A third period is now emerging, however, marked by the concern to release once again "the lyricism of life" in uniting sexuality with the experience of the sacred and of the cosmic order. The concern is prompted by new, more wholistic understandings of the person and of the ways in which sexuality is present in the total range of human experience. If during the second period sexuality (particularly sexual desire) was viewed as a distraction to the life of mind and spirit, now there is a growing recognition that sexuality is so involved in the center of a person's life and of his or her powers of creativity that its denial thwarts the deepest possibilities of human fulfillment. Sexual expression still needs ordering and discipline, yes, but that is quite different from the denial of the spiritual power of sexuality itself.

Already it should be apparent that I am using two key terms rather broadly, and quite deliberately so. By spirituality I mean not only the conscious religious disciplines and practices through which human beings relate to God, but more inclusively the whole style and meaning of our relationship to that which we perceive as of ultimate worth and power. This includes disciplines and practices, but also myths, symbols, and rituals, informal as well as formal. It includes the affective as well as the cognitive. Significantly, spirituality includes the ways in which our relatedness to the ultimate affects our understandings and feelings of relatedness to everyone and everything else.

By sexuality I mean not only physiological arousal and genital activity, but also much more. While human sexuality is not the whole of our personhood, it is a basic dimension of that personhood. While it does not determine all thought, feeling, and action, it does permeate and affect all of these. Sexuality is our way of being in the world as female or male persons. It involves our appropriation of characteristics socially defined as feminine or masculine. It includes our affectional-sexual orientation toward those of the opposite and/or the same sex. It is our attitudes toward ourselves and others as *body*-selves. It is our capacity for sensuousness. It is all of this.

The intimate relation between sexuality and spirituality is evident if one believes, as I do, that sexuality is both a symbol and a means of communication and communion. The mystery of sexuality is the mystery of the human need to reach out for the physical and spiritual embrace of others. Sexuality thus expresses God's intention that people find authentic humanness not in isolation but in relationship. In sum, sexuality always involves much more than what we do with our genitals. More fundamentally, it is who we are as body-selves who experience the emotional, cognitive, physical, and spiritual need for intimate communion, both creaturely and divine.[2]

Perhaps these definitions seem too ideal, belonging to Ricoeur's third period. Realistically, we know that sexual alienation abounds. It is alienation from ourselves (bodies feel foreign, or bodies are used as pleasure machines). It is alienation from others (we fear intimacy and vulnerability; we use sexuality in patterns of domination and submission). It is alienation from God (sexuality seems alien to "true spirituality").

The historical roots of sexual alienation are not difficult to find. They emerged as two intertwining dualisms. Spiritualistic dualism (spirit over body, mind over matter) emerged with power in late Hellenistic Greece and made a lasting impact upon the Christian church. Championed by the Neoplatonists, this dualism viewed the immortal spirit as a temporary prisoner in a mortal, corruptible body. The good life and, indeed, salvation itself required escape from flesh into spirit. Sexist or patriarchal dualism (man over woman) is the twin of spiritualism.

6

While Old Testament life was not strongly marked by spiritualism, patriarchal dualism abounded, and it too found a home in the emerging Christian community. It involved the systematic subordination of women in interpersonal relations, in institutions, in thought forms, and in religious life. But the two dualisms became inextricably intertwined as men assumed to themselves superiority in spirit and reason while identifying women with body, earthiness, irrationality, and instability.

So we Christians today live between the times. Or perhaps we live between the gardens. One garden is the Erotic Garden, that depicted in The Song of Songs. This much-misinterpreted piece of scripture is a biblical love poem celebrating the joys of erotic love between a woman and a man. Even though through much of Christian history it was allegorized into a symbol of the purely spiritual life purged of any carnal reality, the Canticles is a sexual story.

But it is sexuality beyond the fall. In this garden there is no bodily shame. This garden and its inhabitants are thoroughly sensual. The woman and the man delight not only in each other's embodiedness but also in the sensuous delights surrounding them—trees, fruits, flowers, fountains of living water. In this garden there is no sexist dualism, no hint of patriarchy, no dominance or submission. The woman is fully the equal of the man. Independent, she works, takes initiatives, and has an identity of her own apart from her lover. The two alternate in inaugurating their meetings. Each exults in the body and beauty of the other, and together they embrace their sexuality without the guilt of exploitation.

The Garden of Eden depicted in the Yahwist creation story, Genesis 2—3, is different. Here the results of the fall into sexual dualism are evident. There is shame in nakedness. The whole material world participates in the fall. Work itself is cursed and childbirth marked with alienating pain. The writer of this garden story seems to depict the woman as derivative of the man.

In all this there is something of a literary irony. The Garden of Eden, which is mythic, seems to give the more realistic portrayal of the human sexual story, whereas the real historical tale of two lovers, the Canticles, seems to border on sexual myth.[3] Nevertheless, one might ask, which is "realistic," our alienation or our possibility?

If there are two basic traditions regarding sexuality represented in the two gardens—one emphasizing creation and human creative capacity, the other emphasizing the fall and the need for pardon and redemption—there are also two broad tendencies in Western Christian spirituality which have a significant parallel.[4] And it is quite obvious that sin-redemption spirituality has dominated creation-centered spirituality. Furthermore, the domination has been so steady that it has been taken for granted.

The intimate linkage of sin-redemption spirituality with sexual dualism is striking. Its roots in the early Church Fathers and, particularly, in Augustine were sunk in the same soil that nurtured an ongoing Christian commitment to both Hellenistic and patriarchal dualisms. In both literature and practice the dominant Western spirituality denigrated women as less than fully human. In the name of holiness it was deeply suspicious of the human body. It exalted a life devoid of passion. Its focus on salvation history left little thought for nature. It said much about private piety but little about social justice.

Three students of our spirituality traditions speak to these issues. Mary Aileen Schmiel believes that the concentration on a metaphysics of fall-redemption has meant a systematic exile of the positive creative power destined for persons made in the Creator's image.

In adopting a dualistic cosmology, by separating the

City of God from the city of man/woman, we have divorced the law from the spirit, or political justice from religious consciousness. Even within religion, we have concentrated entirely upon "worship," which is directed toward transcendence of everyday life, and excluded celebration, which brings a God-consciousness to earth.[5]

Likewise, Nicolas Berdyaev argues that sin-redemption spirituality has contributed mightily to the split between church and world: the church is seen as concerned with salvation while the world is concerned with creativity. "Salvation is the primary task, the first necessity; creativity is a secondary or tertiary task, a supplement to life, but not its very essence."[6]

The most searing summary indictment of this dominant spirituality remains for Matthew Fox to make:

It has failed to resist docetism and the dehumanizing of Jesus and the incarnation event. In its dualistic view of the world it pits salvation history against history, supernature against nature, soul against body, redemption against creation, artist against intellectual, heaven (and hell) against earth, the sensual against the spiritual, man against woman, individual against society, and condemns all those with a cosmic vision (creation after all *is* cosmic) as pantheists.[7]

The movement toward a more healed, wholistic spirituality and the movement toward a more healed, wholistic sexuality cannot be separated. It is not just that they *ought* not to be separated; quite literally they *cannot* be. One is necessary to the other. They are inseparable elements of full personhood. True, we Christians live between the two gardens. But if our spirituality has been one-sided in its sin-redemption emphasis, the vision of the Erotic Garden might help us. Some comment on several dimensions of a spirituality informed by the garden may illustrate this.[8]

Feeling is one such dimension. Feeling includes emotion, but it is more. It is the wholeness of the human response to reality, involving both cognition and emotion. It is the willingness to respond with as much of the totality of the self as one is able. It is the capacity to be deeply aroused by what one experiences. But feeling is inseparable from the sexual body-self. Both psychologists and psychiatrists give ample testimony that dissociation from one's body and one's sexuality brings with it shallowness of feeling—or even, in a dramatic case such as a schizophrenic episode, the incapacity to feel at all. But when one has a unified sense of the body-self, one is more apt to respond with feeling, for then one can listen to the messages from all the self's aspects: the mind, the heart, the genitals, the viscera, the spiritual sensitivities.

Desire is obvious in sexuality. The Canticles depicts it as a major theme of the Erotic Garden, in which it is evidently the erotic desire of lover for lover. What is less obvious is that desire, erotic desire, is intrinsic to spirituality. More than Roman Catholics, Protestants have been conditioned by understandings of revelation that make the human being into receptor only, a passive, waiting vessel who can only respond to the divine initiative. But this is to impoverish the erotic dimension of knowing another, including knowing God.

The ancient Hebrews knew better when they occasionally used the verb to know as a synonym for sexual intercourse, for the sexual act at its best is the union of desiring and knowing. If I desire another sexually without wanting deep personal knowledge or living communion with the partner, then I treat the other as object, as means to my own gratification. But in the union of desiring and knowing, I treat my partner as a self, the treasured participant in communion. We both know and desire with the same flesh.

If desire is a way to knowledge of another human

being, it is also a pathway to the Holy. Long before the unfortunate theological disjunction between agape and eros, the Hebrew psalmist knew that erotic desire was intrinsic to communion with God: "As a doe longs for running streams, so longs my soul for you, my God. My soul thirsts for God, the God of life [Ps. 42:1–2, JB]." In a similar vein Charles Davis has affirmed the self-transcending power of sexual love: "The erotic dynamism of bodily love is not an arbitrary and somewhat bold and dangerous symbol, but an intrinsic element in the movement of an embodied person in openness toward the plenitude of reality, toward God."[9]

Communion is a term that might almost be synonymous with spirituality. The richest times of spiritual awareness are pervaded by both desire for and experience of communion with God, and hence also with human beings and nature. Affirmation of the sexual dimension of the human relationship with God can assist us, I am convinced, in overcoming that commonly felt subject-object dichotomy in religious experience. In authentic sexual communion with a beloved human partner, whether that communion is genitally expressed or not, the dichotomy between persons is overcome while a rich polarity remains. It is unity, though not unification. Each self respects the other's identity, not confusing it with its own wishes or fantasies, and, in the ecstasy of mutual giving and receiving, creative differences remain.

The sexual experience of overcoming dichotomy without absorption into the human partner is more than simply an analogy for human communion with God. Both are of one piece. One capacity participates in the other. Moreover, an inability to overcome the sense of distance between God and the self means a fading awareness of divine immanence. It is then that God is no longer experienced as vital, indwelling presence permeating the stuff of everyday life. Rather, God seems to be only object opposed to subject. And when immanence fades, God's transcendence also becomes less real.

In Christian liturgy the eucharist (surely *the* sacramental expression of body theology) is the paradigmatic experience of communion, the earthly symbol of the ultimate unity promised to all in God's New Age. In the sacrament individuality is not erased; rather, deeply unique individuals are bonded together. Thus communion, in whatever form, is participation in the other. It is different from possession, wherein I objectify the other and desire control. In participation there is intersubjectivity. Between God and the self there is not just relationship but an interdwelling of personal presences.

Incarnation, as will be discussed in chapter 2, expresses the intimate link between sexuality and spirituality. Indeed, it is the central connection. Human bodies are designed as instruments of communion. There is implanted deep within us an eros, a yearning toward intimate relation. Augustine's well-known prayer put it this way: "Thou hast created us for thyself, O God, so that our hearts are restless until they find their rest in thee." Incarnational theology fully affirms those words. It only wishes to add the clarification that the God toward whom our restlessness presses us is met in flesh. The material body has not only been pronounced good, it has been graced as vehicle of the divine presence.

Christian faith has traditionally affirmed that the incarnation of God in Jesus of Nazareth is the unique, unrepeatable, sufficient revelation. In overstating the case and in shifting the description of the divine-human presence to a metaphysical problem of two natures, however, the tradition has effectively lost the mystery and reality of God's continuing and repeated incarnation in and through human flesh. The paradox is that God's incarnation in Jesus is sufficient only if it nourishes repetition. Jesus as Christ is our faith community's paradigm, our living symbol of God's *ongoing* embodiment—and of the possibility of our being, in some measure, body-words of the divine love.

Finally, *compassion* is integral to spirituality, and it too is intimately related to our sexuality. If the spirituality informed by the Erotic Garden refuses to block out the body, neither will it block out the body politic. While much of Western spirituality has been the quest for individual perfection, compassion demands that spirituality be utterly social and universally embracing. Compassion is not paternalistic pity but rather an egalitarian and passionate caring about persons and institutions. If spirituality means kinship with God, it means kinship with God's universe.

The connection of compassion with sexuality, as Matthew Fox has observed, is captured in the feminist version of the old camp song: "Climbing Jacob's Ladder" has become "Dancing Sarah's Circle."[10] Ladder-oriented spirituality is rooted in the sexual dualisms. Male-dominated religiosity has leaned heavily toward transcendence, movement away from the earth, privatism, and hierarchical organization. Such religiosity, which has denigrated the human body, has not been highly motivated to take on social-justice issues—which, after all, are material and body issues. In contrast, the healing of the body-spirit split and of the man-woman split promises a much more compassionate spirituality. It will be more sensuous and earthy, hence concerned with the interdependence of all things. It will be a dancing, celebrating spirituality that finds works of justice the cause for celebration. It will be a spirituality that challenges the compassionate creativity of the human being.

These, then, are some marks of a spirituality informed by the vision of the Erotic Garden: feeling, desire, communion, incarnation, and compassion. But the movement in this direction needs to be undergirded by changes in Christian community. For one thing, our theology must be resexualized. This does not mean putting sexuality into a theology from which it has been absent, for it has always been there. Rather, it means changes that will overcome the sexual dualisms which have plagued Christian thought. Our understanding of God is the central case in point. Because our imagery and language have been so one-sidedly masculine, a masculinist-shaped spirituality has resulted. Hence we have experienced God dominantly as noun, as transcendence, as order, as structure, as law, as rationality. A more androgynous theological imagery and language will help us to experience God also as verb, as immanence, as creativity, as vulnerability, as flow, and as absolute relatedness to creation.

The affirmation of human sexuality is part and parcel of these latter ways of experiencing God. It is a commonly attested phenomenon that when a person becomes more comfortable and affirmative as a sexual human being (including, to be sure, the sexual celibate), he or she is also more open to a whole range of life's joy and pain. There is a greater capacity to undergo change. Life becomes less static and closed, more dynamic and open. Likewise, when a person is deeply "in love" with another, these things seem to occur also. Perhaps the affirmation of the sexuality present in our love for God and God's love for us can affect us even more grandly with the dynamism of the Cosmic Love.

Not only the theological but also the liturgical life of the Christian community needs resexualizing. Spiritualistic dualism has made the church uneasy about the bodily implications of its worship, having proclaimed the body as incidental to the life and of the spirit. Sexist dualism has masculinized liturgy in both image and language. But the reform of these dualisms can be accompanied by an enhanced recognition of the positive sexual dimensions in Christian liturgical and sacramental life. And the discovery of this in worship can only aid the discovery of the sacramentality that is hidden in human sexuality.

Further, if compassion as social justice is an important mark of Christian spirituality, the church will need to attend more perceptively to the ways in which the unhealed sexual dualisms contribute so heavily to the great social problems of the day. Social violence is but one example. Whether it is violence through crime on the streets or through a world arms race, the sex-role distortions of hypermasculinism are importantly in the picture. And if social violence might be mitigated through greater healing of sexist dualism, it will also be lessened through the healing of body-spirit dualism. Cross-cultural anthropological studies reveal significant links between body repression and social violence in some societies. The opposite is true in others, where there is a positive correlation between bodily affirmation and societal peacefulness.

In any event, the links between sexuality and spirituality are profound. Because the dualisms have done their alienating work so effectively, Christians fail to recognize many of these connections. We do live between the times, and between the two gardens. But the journey of discovery is a promising one for those who believe that the Word is still made flesh in order that we might have life and have it more abundantly.

· 2 ·

Word Becomes Flesh

"Within me even the most metaphysical problem takes on a warm physical body which smells of sea, soil, and human sweat. The Word, in order to touch me, must become warm flesh. Only then do I understand—when I can smell, see, and touch."[1] That, says Nikos Kazantzakis, is our human need.

Rainer Maria Rilke speaks similarly.

> It is certain that the divinest consolation is contained in humanity itself . . . but our eyes should be a shade more perceptive, our ears be more receptive, the taste of a fruit should be absorbed more completely, we should be capable of enduring more intense smells, and be more alert and less forgetful when we touch and are touched—so that in our most immediate experiences we might find consolations which are more convincing, stronger and more valid than the most overwhelming sorrow.[2]

Christian faith answers with a bold affirmation: "In the beginning was the Word, and the Word was with God, and the Word was God. . . . And the Word became flesh and dwelt among us, full of grace and truth [John 1:1, 14]." That is a radical claim, with which the church and countless Christians have struggled over the centuries. It asserts that flesh is important. It says that matter matters.

It declares that a compelling incarnation of God has occurred in a certain human being, one Jesus of Nazareth. And more, it leads to the affirmation that somehow Christian faith at its core is about the embodiment of God in our own daily flesh-and-blood encounters.

With each of the above three assertions there are problems. Christians have difficulty believing that human bodies are important and good, and that they and the whole material world are pregnant with the divine presence. Though Archbishop William Temple could say that Christianity is "the most avowedly materialistic of all the great religions,"[3] we have been sufficiently affected by spiritualistic dualism to distrust that. The regrettable legacy of Hellenistic Greece—the notion that spirit and body are fundamentally different, with spirit the eternal, good reality and body the temporal, lower, even evil part of us—has woven its way into the fabric of our corporate and personal histories.

There is then a two-way problem that arises with our Christology, with our attempts to understand the meanings of God's incarnation. Because we have difficulty accepting the goodness of bodies and matter, we find it difficult to believe that in that compelling instance of God's embrace of humanity—Jesus of Nazareth—God's presence did not in some way eradicate Jesus' genuine humanity. That Jesus should be a laughing, crying, sweating, urinating, defecating, orgasmic, sensuous bundle of flesh just as we are seems incomprehensible. Then the reverse is also true. Because we find it difficult to believe that God genuinely embraced total flesh in Jesus, we have trouble believing that incarnation can and does occur in us too. Lacking the conviction that God not only blesses human flesh from afar but also intimately embraces and permeates the body-selves which we are, expressing divine presence and activity in the world through us, we find it difficult to incorporate our sexuality into our spirituality.

17

But if we do not know the gospel in our bodies, we do not know the gospel. We either experience God's presence in our bodies or not at all. If the gospel is not fundamentally an idea but an action, a deliverance, and if no action can be bodiless in human experience, the gospel must bring good news and liberation to our bodies or it will not liberate anything.[4]

Perhaps Norman O. Brown was right: "The last thing to be realized is the incarnation. The last mystery to be unveiled is the union of humanity and divinity in the body."[5] And the last thing to be realized is that the Word, God's dynamic, life-shaping presence, not only *became* flesh two millennia ago but also *becomes* flesh now. If it is true for Christians that believing the former is crucial for experiencing the latter, it may, paradoxically, be just as true that without the experience of the latter—God's present embodiment in our sisters, our brothers, and ourselves—beliefs about Jesus as Christ become abstract formulas with little connection to life.

But there is another possibility. And to explore that I turn to body theology.

The Body in Christian Theology

Fresh concerns about the body are emerging in Christian theology and ethics from a variety of sources. Feminist theology is exposing the pervasive ways in which sexism alienates both women and men from their bodies. Lesbians and gay males are insisting on the significance of their own body experience for Christian theology. Third-world liberationists are asserting that theology's primary task is to change social structures that dehumanize and bodily oppress the poor. Ecological theology is recognizing the intimate connections between our bodies and the earth. Medical ethics is showing new concern for wholistic health care that attends to the body-spirit unity of persons.[6]

While spiritualistic dualism and its companion, patriarchal or sexist dualism, have tragically marred Christian life and thought through the centuries, it is not fair to say that the view of the body in Christian religious tradition has been totally or consistently negative. In addition to the admittedly negative views of the body as foil for the soul and the body as an intrinsic detriment to true spirituality, there were positive perceptions in the early Christian era, as historian Margaret R. Miles has discovered. True, early asceticism frequently fell into the dualistic assumptions of a closed energy system, with the soul gathering energy at the expense of the body. Such asceticism also frequently succumbed to a punitive orientation, wherein the body was punished so that the self as a whole might be spared divine punishment. As Miles points out, however, "Neither discipline nor punishment is the goal of asceticism, but rather freeing of the body from the stranglehold of the [alienated] flesh so that it can come to share in the life and energy of the spirit."[7]

Gnosticism was a constant threat to early Christian understanding. The Gnostics believed that incarnation was evil, matter was evil, and the true home of the human spirit lay in the spiritual world released from the snares of body and matter. While gnosticism made some inroads into the early church, most Christians seemed to realize that the affirmations of the goodness of creation, of the incarnation, and of the resurrection of the body required them to reject such teachings.

In later centuries there are additional evidences of positive attitudes toward the physical. When interest in speculative theology was lost in the early Middle Ages, there arose a marked interest in the practical expressions of incarnation. Because God had become incarnate in

Jesus, the divine power could even now be expected in the material world—in spontaneous, unpredictable eruptions. Thus there was great interest in miracles, in physical healings, in relics and saints, and in the capacity of holy objects, places, and people to express and mediate the divine power.[8] And in the thirteenth century lived Francis of Assisi, "the last and greatest medieval Christian to understand the world within the incarnational framework."[9] To Francis, God was directly and immediately present in the material world. The world of matter and the senses was the *form* in which God might be known and loved. Such a physical world was not to be seen as a distraction from God but rather as precisely the arena in which the divine presence could be discerned.

In spite of these positive moments of incarnational embrace, in spite of the biblical teaching that the body is "a temple of the Holy Spirit [1 Cor. 6:19]," our religious tradition overall has shown marked ambivalence about the physical. Christian faith has been more commonly interpreted as the realm of "the spiritual," and the spiritual has been assumed to be nonmaterial, nonbodily. The result is that theology's concern with the body is with what it might say *about* the body, with the assumption that theology somehow emerges from a superior, nonphysical vantage point. But what if the incarnation is pervasively true—that God is met bodily if God is met at all? Then body experience is not somehow lower than spiritual experience, nor does theology start somewhere else and then speak about the body's proper (disciplined and subordinate) place in the scheme of things. Rather, incarnational theology itself must be a body theology.

The Body as Relation to God

It is important to acknowledge that the unity of the body-self is always problematic.[10] Even in good physical health we human beings sense the fragility of our unity. On the one hand, how can we be anything other than bodies? Though our language itself bears signs of alienation (it seems more natural to say "I have a body" than to say "I am a body"), is not the union between my body and me profoundly intimate? Yet I also experience the body's strangeness. Though I can express myself only through my body, I am limited by it at every turn: by its finite location in space (if I am here, I am not there); by the ways my emotions either seem blocked within body prisons or seem to run their bodily course quite apart from my conscious will; by the constant threat of disability, illness, and ultimately death.

Thus, I live with a paradox that I cannot escape: my body is me, yet not me. As Richard Zaner says, "Compellingly mine, it is yet radically other: intimately alien, strangely mine. Most of all, my body is the embodiment of that most foreign of all things—death."[11] Yearning to transcend our mortality, we yet recognize the body as bearer of mortality itself. Human beings are, as Ernest Becker has graphically said, "gods with anuses."[12]

Christians face, then, a double problem. Under the impact of spiritualistic dualism in our tradition, we have learned to suspect and fear the body. But, in addition to what we have been taught, our experience itself can make the body-self unity problematic. Does a body theology then make any sense? Indeed, it does. In fact, there is nowhere else to begin. If some theologians seem to attempt to see and speak from God's point of view, other theologians find only impossibility and folly in such attempts. There is no way bodily concreteness and particularity can be transcended in religious reflection. But these limitations are actually an incarnational gift.

Body theology is not simply a theological description of the body (as if there were some superior vantage point from which to view it). Nor is such theology simply an

21

attempt to understand the body as housing of the soul. Nor is it a matter of designing rules for bodily life. Rather, it affirms that bodily experience must be the starting point for any theological reflection at all.[13]

The concreteness of the world is nourishing in a way that abstractions are not, as Emily Gibbs realizes in the "resurrection" scene in Thornton Wilder's *Our Town:* "Grover's Corners . . . Mama and Papa . . . clocks ticking . . . and Mama's sunflowers. And food and coffee. And new-ironed dresses and hot baths . . . and sleeping and waking up. Oh, earth, you're too wonderful for anybody to realize you."[14]

It is that kind of concreteness with which body theology begins. It is also the concreteness of the genetically deformed infant born to grieving young parents. It is the late-night phone call bearing a suicide threat. It is the Lebanese or Salvadoran child whose sad eyes speak of lost innocence amid violent surroundings. It is the concreteness of hardened concrete in missile silos. Body theology begins with all this experience.

But what does body experience mean? Upon reflection we realize that our bodies are not simply objects, for they are our special and only means of knowing what any object in the world is like.[15] We know, for example, that we locate all physical objects *in relation to* our bodies. Our use of prepositions in speech—in, over, under, between, behind, beyond, beside, within, without—depends on our instinctive sense of our own bodily location in relation to the rest of our experienced world. Indeed, through our bodies we learn that the fundamental reality with which we deal is not simply living beings as such, nor objects as such, but rather it is relationships.

Body meaning, however, does not come through relationships as such, but through *personal* relationships. Without the humanizing process of touch, speech, and gesture from other persons, the infant would not learn personal meaning. The presence of another person (when I recognize the other *as* person and not simply as object) makes me want to communicate. The presence of the other makes me want to interpret myself—and I quite literally do not know who I am until I try to explain myself.

The discovery human beings make very early in life, much earlier than our ability to articulate it, is that genuinely personal presence is life-giving. The relationship with another who is responding to me in ways that take my personhood seriously elicits my sense of well-being, my creativity, my capacity for reciprocity, my desire to care.

There is an awesomeness, a mystery about the presence of another in personal relationship. There is something there which neither person has created. The relationship itself has a gift quality about it. The religiously sensitive throughout the ages have identified this experience as encounter with the divine. Thus Martin Buber says that in every true meeting of the I and the thou, there is the Thou. Likewise, H. Richard Niebuhr discerns all interpersonal reality as triadic in nature. The self in relation to the neighbor is always related because of God, and the self's relation to God (even in physical solitude) is always experienced with the compresence of the neighbor.

Thus, we know God not in some kind of divine aseity (Godself alone, unrelated to us or to anything else). We know God only in relationship. Buber put it this way: "In the beginning is the relation."[16] The beginning for us is not one presence, not even God. Insofar as it has any meaning to us at all, the relationship is fundamental.[17]

This has important implications for the whole task of theology. Most simply, theology is what the church teaches (or ought to teach) about God. But if God is known only in relationship, then the task of theology is the attempt, in the community of faith, to express the meanings of God *in relation* to the world.

This means that it is not theology's principal task to interpret scripture or to transmit the tradition. Rather, its principal task is to clarify within the community of faith the experience of God in relatedness to us—with the aids of scripture and tradition. Post-Enlightenment, liberal theology may have its problems, but its central insights are of enormous importance. It maintains that the experience of the world is the primary arena of divine activity for us. This runs counter to the tendency to locate God primarily outside the world, outside the body, outside the present; and inside the Bible, inside the church, inside heaven, inside the past or the future.[18]

As human beings experience a personal presence in the world, and as that presence is life-giving, we are moved to name it God. And we recognize that the experience of personal presence is always voluntary. There is nothing automatic about it. I can choose to respond to another human being as a personal "thou" or as an impersonal "it." So also the Jewish and Christian traditions speak of the relation between God and humanity throughout history as a voluntary personal relation. The covenant between Yahweh and Israel has nothing predetermined about it. Yahweh speaks, the Israelities respond—or fail to respond. There is a relational power that the people are free to claim or reject.

Christology as Interpretation of Jesus and Our Bodily Experience

The purpose of Christology in Christian doctrine usually has been understood to focus solely on the meeting of the divine and the human in Jesus of Nazareth. Thus a standard theological dictionary says, "Christology is the attempt to clarify the elemental confession of Christian faith, that Jesus is the Christ. . . . The doctrine of the Trinity serves to clarify the christological affirmation of the divinity (or deity) of Christ. . . . Christology shifts the focus to Jesus Christ. It inquires how it is *in Jesus Christ* that God is present and active with us. The inquiry thus becomes centred on the relation between the divine and the human in this person."[19]

I would argue, however, that this is too narrow. By literal insistence or by implication, mainstream theological tradition has confined the Christ to Jesus. In so doing, the practical effect has been to deny the reality of the christic experience and power to everyone else. More adequately, the purpose of Christology is to attempt to understand Jesus as Christ *and also* to understand and affirm God's incarnate, relational activity in human life in the present and in the future.[20]

If the experience of personal presence in the meeting with another is voluntary (nothing automatic, nothing predetermined, nothing foreordained), this gives an important clue to the nature of incarnation. As incarnation applies to Jesus, that reality resulted from voluntary choice. Jesus could have decided otherwise. He was not fated to be our messiah. He could have chosen to resist God's radical claim of love. In fact, he chose to open himself to that claim. He chose to respond with all the fullness of being of which he was capable.

The understanding of divine incarnation as a voluntary experience, however, has been a precarious one in the Christian tradition.[21] Under the influence of Greek philosophy, the church lost much of its sense of the free quality of the relationship between the divine and the human. In order to preserve the humanity and divinity of Jesus as Christ, the Council of Chalcedon (A.D. 451) rejected the Antiochene Christology that suggested a personal, moral relation between the human Jesus and the divine God. Instead, the church substituted a hypostatic or essential union of the two natures.

The implication of Chalcedon was that the human and

divine natures were so distinctly "other" that there was possible no voluntary cooperation between them. Thus in Jesus it was not a meeting of love between divinity and humanity. Rather, the notion of a personal, moral relation was replaced by a conception of ontological union: the divine and the human were united "without confusion, without change, without separation." Divinity dominated humanity, relegating it to the realm of that which needed to be overcome.

A view of Christ emerged that was once-and-for-all. Incarnation was confined to that one individual. Here was a being with whom Christians might have a transactional relationship through faith, but not one who was ours to incorporate in the most intimate, personal, bodily experience. What was substituted was the belief in an unchanging God of perfection, one whose divine love was completely other than human love, whose divine being was completely other than human bodily being. Lost was the compelling experience of the incarnate God as the meaning, the reality, and the power of our relationship to other created beings. Lost was the life-giving experience of knowing God as the inmost presence and power of our own being.

When salvation history was centered in the person of Jesus as *the* Christ, the door was opened to oppressive implications. Subsequent Christian theology lent itself all too frequently to the oppression of the Jews, for if Jesus is the only and true messiah then the Jewish people are spiritually blind in their scriptural exegesis and piety, and their divine reprobation is justified.[22] Such Christology has all too frequently been oppressive to women, inasmuch as it became linked to the maleness of Jesus and the maleness of the Father God.[23] By affirming Jesus as Christ to be "the center of all things," such Christology has "rendered weak, invisible, or ashamed by the church's affirmation" countless persons who are not male, not white, or who are Semitic, or who are born without inheritance, or who are without community, or who feel strongly about their sexuality. For all these persons sense their significant difference from that one person who has been claimed to be the only Christ.[24] Such Christology has paved the way for "triumphalist" theologies and the superior posturing of the Christian church in relation to any and all who are "outside the covenant." It has contributed to a theological defense of reactionary and oppressive politics.[25]

And in all this, human bodily experience seems distant from God.

Orthodox Christology, however, was attempting to grapple with an affirmation of enormous importance: the source of salvation is in God. If the two great christological councils of the church, Nicaea and Chalcedon, insisted on the divinity of Jesus, it was because these early Christians were convinced that the power to make alive, to reconcile, to redeem was God's power. The regrettable fact was that the orthodox formulations led to a view of humanity that emphasized passivity and powerlessness. The formulas have led countless Christians to believe that there is really only one God-bearing person to be encountered in human history, and that is Jesus. All others are excluded from the christic nature.[26]

What if Christians believe that the desire of God is that all human beings—not just one—be Christ-bearers? What if we believe that the Love that (as Dante said) "moves the sun and the other stars" deeply yearns for intimate union with every person, desiring that each one participate in the redemption of the world? Then we who stake our claims with the Christian community and its tradition find in Jesus of Nazareth the crucial paradigm of the Christ. But this paradigmatic figure does not monopolize the Christ. Indeed, his purpose is precisely the opposite: to free and to release the christic reality that it might be embodied in the fleshly relationships of all. Norman Pittenger puts it well: "If Jesus released the divine love into human life in an unprecedented manner and degree, he did this because in all respects he shared the [humanity] which is ours; and if we, in our turn, can appropriate that love released in his accomplishment, it is because it was disclosed and made effective in those very human terms which are also ours."[27]

Incarnation—personal presence—is a voluntary process. Jesus was free to reject the intimate union with God, as are we. But he chose to respond to that presence, and in the process both he and God were changed. Something new was revealed about both God's presence and human presence. In Carter Heyward's words, "And the something new—the revelation—is that when God and humanity act together in the world, human action and divine action are the same action, the same love, the same justice, the same power, the same peace."[28]

Incarnation is always a paradox of grace.[29] Indeed, the experience of grace, God's love in action, is always paradoxical in human experience. We recognize that the best we are and do ultimately has its source beyond us in God. At the same time our lives and our actions are never more truly personal, responsible, and free than when their divine source is affirmed. Paul expresses the paradox in saying, "I worked harder than any of them, though it was not I, but the grace of God which is with me [1 Cor. 15:10]." Thus we cannot draw any sharp boundary line between God's work and our own, between God's action and our action. Both sides of the paradox are true and need to be affirmed. It is false to say that the more of God's grace there is in an action, the less it is my own action. More truly, it is the other way around. The deepest paradox of the Christian religion is the incarnational one.

Incarnation is a miracle. Yet the essence of the miraculous is not the interference in the natural world by the supernatural, but the authentic discovery of who we are. As H.A. Williams puts it,

> The discovery is miraculous because the previous organization of our being provided no vantage point from which we could have seen what we now do see. . . . I find that I am both more and other than I had previously imagined. And this discovery of myself is invariably accompanied by the kindred discovery that I belong intimately to the world in which I live and which I now feel belongs to me.[30]

Such discoveries are never once and for all. They are luminous moments in an ongoing process, moments that shed light upon the meaning of all else.

The Word became flesh. And the Word continues to become flesh. Both meanings of incarnation are important. If we affirm only the first, we drastically diminish the religious value of all the rest of human history.[31] Moreover, we are led to think of incarnation as possession more than as relationship. And we deny the reality of the present embodiment of God, the indwelling of Christ. But if we affirm only present incarnation and neglect the reality of the Christ in Jesus, we lose the power of that particularly luminous moment in our communal history. We lose the transformative power of that paradigmatic one to nourish and shape the embodied God in us. Both meanings are important.

Resurrection of the Body: Incarnation and Our Sexuality

If the Word continues to become flesh, if bodily experience is crucial to the experience of divine presence, the connections with human sexuality may be obvious. Yet in

29

life the obvious is often the most difficult to grasp in our experience. This seems particularly true with our sexuality, marred as it is by the dualisms of the centuries and the continuing legacy of ignorance, fear, and guilt. To explore various facets of our incarnational-sexual experience is the purpose of the essays in this book. But, by way of further groundwork—and in light of the previous affirmations about body life, relatedness, and God—consider these possibilities:

- that our body experience might express God's hunger,
- that our body experience might express God's language,
- that our body experience might express God's interrelatedness with all else,
- and that it might express the divine pleasure.

God's hunger. When the author of the Fourth Gospel spoke of the Word becoming flesh, that writer was utilizing the Greek concept of the Logos as "Word." The term Logos was introduced into Greek philosophy by Heraclitus of Ephesus in the fifth century B.C.[32] Prior to Heraclitus the nature of reality was believed to be static and mathematical, but in this philosopher's vision the cosmos was in ceaseless change; one could never step into the same river twice. The cosmos was a state of becoming. But if that becoming were not to result in chaos there must be an intelligent, eternal power that guided change into order and meaning.

John B. Cobb Jr. describes it this way: "The Logos is the cosmic principle of order, the ground of meaning, and the source of purpose, . . . the lure for feeling, the eternal urge of desire, the divine Eros."[33] Cobb's description conveys the religious insight that the Logos is not fundamentally abstract, rational power, but is more truly that dynamic, ordering will which is marked by passion and desire—indeed, by hunger. This is the nature of that Word which becomes flesh: a hunger for wholeness.

Classical theology, which dominated the church's thought for centuries, finds this all quite foreign. In that tradition, God is totally complete, forever fulfilled, and has no intrinsic need of human beings or anything else in creation. There is no hunger. "At best," as Bernard Lee has observed, "God takes dessert to be polite."[34] In recent decades, however, a more biblical perception of the God who changes, who yearns, who is incomplete without the embrace of creaturely life has been rediscovered, particularly through process theology. No longer is it adequate to embrace those ancient philosophical categories which assumed that God was immutable and changeless, that God could only give but not receive, that God could only cause effects but could not be affected.

God is marked by eros as well as agape. And what is eros? It is "the life instinct, the large sense of the passionate drive for life and growth, and the power of those passionate instincts that derives from their satisfaction."[35] It may well be, then, that the human experience of eros is a crucial arena for meeting God. It may be that our genuine human hungers are experiences of the divine hunger. We know these experiences bodily—with our sexual bodies.

Surely one of the central meanings of sexuality is the yearning for reunion, the appetite for wholeness that can be satisfied only in intimacy with others. The word sexuality itself comes from the Latin verb *secare*, meaning to cut or divide. The word suggests the primitive human sense that we experience separation and long for reunion with the entirety of our body-selves. Observations of people in public places, the reading of gossip magazines, overhearing ordinary conversations all reveal the ways in which people are excited by and energized by other people. "This," as Richard Rohr accurately comments, "is sexuality. It is our energy for life and for communication. Without it, we would settle for a cold metallic kind of life. . . . The power of bonding, linkage, and compassion would be gone from the earth."[36]

While sexual arousal and genital desire are only one part of a much richer human sexuality, these experiences can be bodily experiences of God's hunger. To be sure, our sexual arousal and desires can find destructive expressions. But, as Henry Nelson Wieman has suggested, at best they seem intended to break through our confining egoisms, to make us profoundly responsive not only to the other but to all the other's interests and relations. Sexual arousal, in Wieman's view, can be sacramental precisely because it is the experience of greatly heightened human responsiveness and the intense desire to relate.[37]

In James Joyce's *Ulysses*, Molly's "Yes" is this experience: ". . . and then I asked him with my eyes to ask again yes and then he asked me would I yes . . . and first I put my arms around him yes and drew him down to me so he could feel my breasts all perfume yes and his heart was going like mad and yes I said yes I will Yes."[38] We human beings know in our own sexual experience something of Molly's Yes. But Molly is not only us. Molly is also the hungering, passionate God who meets us bodily.

God's language. Logos is translated as Word. That is significant. Humans experience the eternal will to order and meaning, the divine eros, the infinite desire, as Word, language, communication. We are creatures of language. We would not be human without it.[39]

But language is not only vocal or written speech, it is also body language. The parallels between speech and body language are striking, as are those between speech and our sexual meanings. Consider these:

- Speech is physiologically based, but its meanings are culturally determined. That is also true of human sexuality.

- As audible sounds or as written symbols, words have no particular meaning in and of themselves, but are given meaning by the power of human beings in relation to each other. The same is true of our sexual expressions.
- Human language is propositional and syntactical, needing organic units of words and linguistic contexts in order for meanings to be conveyed and understood; the same word in a different linguistic context can mean something quite different. Our sexual acts have a similar character.
- The meanings of human words are never static, but change over time; new words are added to our language, other words fall into disuse, and still other words change in their nuances. The same is true of sexual meanings.
- In simple societies, language patterns are also simpler, and there is more social consensus about language meanings; in complex, pluralistic societies there are varieties of language subgroups, and even the dominant language is susceptible of numerous dialects and accents. This is true of sexual meanings as well.

It is useful, then, to understand human sexuality as a form of language.[40] Sexual behavior is one basic way people have of saying what they mean—or of misleading themselves and others. André Guindon in *The Sexual Language* observes that sexual behavior as language conveys our most intimate understandings of bodily existence. In such speaking, sexual meanings take on a certain originality, a newness. If, however, our sexual language (our bodily words) are nothing but the patterned repetition of someone else's words, our language gradually becomes meaningless. It is a dead tongue. Such disintegration, Guindon notes, can occur through either side of the body-spirit sexual dualism. Spiritualism would rather that the word not become flesh, while corporealism wants the flesh without word. In either case, sexuality loses its human meaning and ceases to be a fundamental medium of truthful communication.[41]

God's language remains abstract, unreal, and ineffectual to us until it becomes embodied. But when the divine Word is embodied it communicates with life-giving power. Speech then becomes quite literally "being in touch." This was what the early church experienced in Jesus as Christ. They experienced him as both body and language. In him they found true language (the universal Word of God) and true bodiliness converging in a single life.

To be sure, human language is always ambiguous. It is false as well as true. It is dangerous as well as life-giving. Our verbal speech creates a world of products that outrun our control and manipulate us. "All the great dangers threatening humanity with extinction," comments Konrad Lorenz, "are direct consequences of conceptual thought and verbal speech."[42] But language is also the basis for transformation of the world. "From the same mouth come blessing and cursing [James 3:10]."

The Word, however, is true. The Word is life-giving. The Word is transforming. And when that Word becomes flesh in human beings, our bodies speak God's language. For the fundamental purpose of language is communication. The fundamental purpose of communication is communion. And communion is the essential meaning of our sexuality.

God's interrelatedness with all. God's bodily speech intends communion—shalom, interconnectedness, interdependence, mutuality of relationship. On the one hand, bodies are means to such relationships. Humans need bodily apparatus complete with vocal cords in order to speak; we need hands to write. With our bodies we enter the relationships that sustain and give meaning to our lives.

But they are not only means to relationships. Our bodies themselves are divine revelations of the interrelatedness of all with all.[43] Though our minds are still saturated with the dualism conveyed by Greek Hellenism, Newtonian science, and Cartesian philosophy—the fundamental split between mind and matter—there is a different vision: that our bodies themselves are revelations of the inclusive community.

Each of us is made up of more than a trillion individual cells, all attempting to work together and maintain one another. Our bodies are communities with their own ventilation systems, sewage systems, communication systems, heating units, and a billion miles of interconnecting streets and alleys.

Our bodies are not only communities in themselves but, even more, communities in relationship with the earth. Our bodily fluids carry the same chemicals as the primeval seas. Quite literally, we carry those seas within ourselves. Our bones contain the same carbon as that which forms the rock of the oldest mountains. Our blood contains the sugar that once flowed in the sap of now-fossilized trees. The nitrogen which binds our bones together is the same as that which binds nitrates to the soil.

Our bodies tell us that we are *one* with the whole earth. Our bodies are revelations of God's new heaven and new earth. And, when cancer eats at our vitals, when bones become brittle and break, when genetic diseases deform innocent infants, there is still revelation in the midst of tragedy. There is still revelation because we know that it was not meant to be this way. The tragic is tragic precisely because it takes its meaning from a vision of harmony and interconnectedness. Such is the body's testimony to the shalom of the New Age where the wolf and lamb shall lie down together.

Teilhard de Chardin puts it provocatively:

The prevailing view has been that the body . . . is a

fragment of the Universe, a piece completely detached from the rest and handed over to a spirit that informs it. In the future we shall have to say that the Body is the very Universality of things. . . . My own body is not these cells or those cells that belong *exclusively* to me: it is *what*, in these cells *and* in the rest of the world feels my influence and reacts against me. *My* matter is not a *part* of the Universe that I possess *totaliter:* it is the *totality* of the Universe possessed by me *partialiter.*"[44]

God's pleasure. In spite of the pain of the alienated dimensions of human sexuality, our bodies furnish us with considerable pleasure. But the suspicion of pleasure is still strong among Christians. One strand of this, undoubtedly, is the parental fear that if children discover sexual pleasure there will be no stopping them short of promiscuity and pregnancy. Beyond this there is simply a strong antipleasure bias in parts of our religious tradition.

From whence did this cloud of churchly suspicion descend on us? Probably from a variety of sources in the long history of the church. The Stoics, who influenced much early Christianity, sought a life devoid of passion. Indeed, some early Stoical Christians wished that the act of intercourse necessary for procreating the race were as devoid of passion as was urination. Medieval theologians were suspicious of orgasm, for at the peak of sexual pleasure people seem to lose their rationality, and to the medievalist rationality was absolutely essential. The Calvinists were convinced that everything must be done decently and in good order, and decency and good order did not seem to leave much room for exuberant sexual pleasure. The Victorians simply assumed that sexual pleasure was animalistic. Even now those Christians who pronounce sex to be holy and good still leave the subject of pleasure largely unexplored and unaffirmed, with the persistent fear that the bold affirmation of sexual pleasure will invite self-indulgence and destroy true spirituality and communion.

But what is sexual pleasure?[45] It is more than just good feelings. It is the union of bodily, emotional, mental, and spiritual feelings in ways that we humans experience markedly positive sensations about the self. In sexual pleasure—be it lovemaking's orgasmic climax or in the deeply sensuous experience of breast-feeding one's infant—the body-self feels profoundly unified, taken out of itself into another, yet intensely itself. There comes a self-abandonment. The ego surrenders some of its control.

Pleasure seems to elude us when we most directly try to produce it. It is denied to the egotist. To have pleasure one must let go, a paradox reflected in Jesus' words about losing life and finding life. Bodily pleasure has the capacity to contribute significantly to human wholeness, and consistent deprivation of genuine bodily pleasure is predictably an invitation to violence.

If genuine bodily pleasure is important to wholeness and communion, why do those syndromes persist that announce, "If it feels good it must be wrong," or "If it hurts, it must be God's will"? One reason, surely, is that much Christian theology and piety has lost touch with the pleasure-giving, pleasure-receiving God. But the Old Testament is full of the One who exults in the sensuous glory of creation and who wills shalom, that rich harmony of peace, justice, joy, and pleasure. And the portrait of Jesus in the New Testament is far removed from that of the stern, body-denying ascetic. Later Christianity, however, in taking the cross as its central symbol, frequently misinterpreted it in ways that exalted pain, suffering, and death when the purpose of Jesus' crucifixion was really to put an end to all crucifixion and to usher in a new age of shalom.[46]

Christians might do well to recapture some of the old

language of the prayer books: "It was God's pleasure to take on our human flesh." And it continues to be God's pleasure to do so, for in embodying the divine presence God expresses the eternal eros, the eternal desire to communicate, the cosmic yearning for the wholeness and interrelatedness of all with all.

That is why faith perceives that the Word not only became but also *becomes* flesh. And that is why W.H. Auden ended his Christmas oratorio, *For the Time Being*, with these words: "Love God in the World of the Flesh; And at your marriage all its occasions shall dance for joy."[47]

· 3 ·

On Men's Liberation

*T*he impact of the feminist movement in recent years has been considerable. In spite of disappointing setbacks, in spite of the massive weight of continuing injustices, gains for women have been real. But the payoffs for men are sometimes negligible, even for those sympathetic to the movement. Male feminists are often lumped together with other males as the oppressor class. They are chided for slips in language. They still mow the lawn and maintain the car while now sharing in the housework. In many fields their job opportunities are diminished. And they often feel kicked simply for being the kind of men they were taught to be. So the confusion, frustration, and anger occasionally surface.

Furthermore, in spite of their efforts to change, they still feel an agonizing kinship with "the loneliness of the long-distance runner," as described by Allan Sillitoe in his book by that title.

> All I knew was that you had to run, run, run, without knowing why you were running, but on you went, through fields you didn't understand and into woods that made you afraid, over hills without knowing you'd been up and down, and shooting across streams that would have cut the heart out of you had you fallen into them. And the winning post was no

end to it, even though the crowds might be cheering you in, because on you had to go.[1]

One of the many gifts of the women's movement to men is the reminder that telling personal stories and reflecting on them can be healing and empowering. For Christians reared on the Bible, this should not have been a surprising discovery, for above all the Bible is a story. Yet the rationalism of male-conditioning has caused many of us to forget.

Well, what is our story? It may be best not to try to tell *our* story, but *my* story—not because the story of this particular middle-aged, white, midwestern, middle-class and privileged American male is so inherently interesting or unique, but simply because it is the story he knows best. And I hope it may have its points of connection with that of the reader.

I was born in 1930 in my parents' bedroom in a small Minnesota town, the third child of second-generation Scandinavian-Americans. The middle child, a girl, died in infancy, leaving my older brother and me. It was a stable, hardworking, and respectable family, attempting to live up to its Presbyterian convictions.

As I look back now, I see how utterly stereotypical my parents' sex roles were. My father was unquestionably the head of the family. As one of the eldest siblings of a twelve-child family of immigrant Norwegian parents, he had been unable to attend college, but had to find employment immediately after high school. He went to work in one of the local banks and stayed there throughout his life, becoming its president as well as a leader in church and community. The clearest messages I remember receiving from him were such as these: always do your best; there is room at the top; a job worth doing is worth doing well; compete and try to win, but always play fair; be a man; big boys don't cry.

My mother is a lovely woman: soft, nurturing, and utterly devoted to her family, her church, and her friends. If the messages received from my father were largely those of *doing*, those from my mother were largely ones of *being*. They were less exhortations to achievement than to the virtues of thoughtfulness, responsibility, helpfulness, and kindness. Occasionally the messages from my two parents did not seem to mesh neatly. When that happened I suspect I leaned toward those from my father.

During the years of public school I tried to live out those injunctions. Do your best (you will get a dime for every *A* on the report card). Be popular (get elected to class offices). Play hard, play fair, and try to win (football is a game of life). Control your feelings (if you can't say anything nice, don't say anything at all). And remember that big boys don't cry (a lesson brought home to me at age five in a stern paternal reprimand for crying when I broke my arm).

The story in college was much the same. My interest in the opposite sex, having gathered force in high school, was now in full bloom. In other ways, too, I found college an exciting adventure and time of achievement, and I was graduated a year ahead of my entering class. I immediately enrolled in law school, perhaps (more than I realized) to fulfill my father's dream. He had deeply desired to be a lawyer, but limited educational opportunities had prevented that. Within three weeks of my having begun law school, however, it became quite clear to me that I was in the wrong place. I quit abruptly, and soon thereafter enlisted in the army. The Korean War was on, and as a nonpacifist I had become increasingly uncomfortable about the academic deferment system. A few weeks later in a basic-training camp in California I received word that my father had had a serious heart attack. Not long thereafter, word came that a second attack in the hospital had caused his death. I had never seen him ill, nor did I have the chance to say goodbye. It was not until a quarter of a century later that it dawned on me that my father's death and my quitting law school were so close in time to each other. (While I do not assume a cause-and-effect relationship, it strikes me as curious that I never in all those years put those two events together.)

A very good college friend, Wilys Claire Coulter, had now become a serious romantic interest, and we were married during the last year of my army enlistment. By this time I had made a decision to attend seminary, not so much to embark on a clergy vocation (for which I then had little interest) as to explore my own questions of faith. So, a few months after my army discharge, we traveled to New Haven, Connecticut, so I might begin theological studies at Yale. Originally I had thought this might be a brief period of exploration. In fact, it lasted for six years.

The early years of our marriage, by any reasonable standards, were generally happy and exciting. Yet there was an undercurrent of strain and bewilderment. We both wanted a marriage of equality, but the traditional sex roles to which we had been conditioned were still very strong. How could I affirm our equality and still be the leader of this partnership? Somehow I knew I wanted both.

In our fourth year of marriage our first child, Steve, arrived, and I well remember my enormous satisfaction that the firstborn was a son. Two weeks later Wilys Claire reentered the hospital for an emergency appendectomy. I was left with Steve, totally unprepared for this full-service parenting role now suddenly thrust upon me. Without repeated appeals to the pages of Dr. Spock and to several neighbors, Steve and I might not have survived. Eighteen months later Mary was born, and I was delighted that we now had "one of each," and all was complete.

In the two parishes to which I later ministered I found great satisfactions and, I hope, some effectiveness in the clergy role. But as I now look back upon my pastoral style,

I am amazed to recognize how traditionally masculinist it was. I was constantly striving for competence, and, yes, excellence. I took seriously the rule of thumb prescribing twenty hours for preparation of a twenty-minute sermon. I tried faithfully to be an available spiritual resource for others, but could not share my own doubts, struggles, and journey. I stood close by while others cried, but never cried with them. And I seldom took a day off.

When later the invitation to join a seminary faculty came, the same tapes continued to play in my head. I now needed to catch up on everything in my field that had been published since graduate-school days. I needed to write the best possible lectures, to be available to students at all hours, and to accept numerous invitations for off-campus speaking. After a couple of years of this, tired and sitting on an airplane returning from a lecture engagement, I was plagued by a mild but persistent nausea. My body was speaking its mind. Then and there I knew I could not live long with that stress and needed help. Not many days later I made my first visit to a therapist's office. I remember my first sentence to him: "I know that you and I are of different faiths—you are Jewish and I am Christian—but I think you will understand when I say that my basic problem is that I simply do not know the meaning of justification by grace."

By then, in the early 1960s, the civil rights movement was gathering force. As a concerned white liberal I tried to do my part. There were two periods of voter registration in Mississippi, including some anxious encounters with a repressive white police system. With the onset of the Vietnam War, I did my share of speaking and picketing. In these ways and others I saw myself as a socially sensitive activist.

The women's movement, however, caught me totally unprepared. I was startled to discover, in an article by Valerie Saiving, the argument that virtually all theology read within the church had been written by males, and that while it purported to describe the universal human situation, it really reflected the male experience.[2] Saiving took on one of my heroes, Reinhold Niebuhr, and with her deft scalpel cut into his major theological formulations to lay bare their masculine bias. Such an awareness was entirely new to me.

About the same time our seminary was enrolling a few women students. Several of them were becoming radicalized by a new feminist consciousness. So also were Wilys Claire and our daughter, Mary. Mary was discovering that even junior-high girls were oppressed in a sexist society. These women began to confront with painful regularity my language, my patterns of thought, my values, my ways of looking at the world. My liberal facade was developing some deep cracks.

A further jolt came with the rise of the gay-lesbian movement. Through involvement in some community action programs, for the first time I was encountering self-affirming, self-respecting, and proud homosexual persons claiming to be fully Christian. I had to confront my own ignorance, my uncritical acceptance of false myths and stereotypes, and my deeply conditioned homophobia. The cracks in my liberalism were growing wider.

In the summer of 1976, with a close friend and colleague, I went to a week's workshop at California's Esalen Institute. It was late June, and I was exhausted. I do not recall ever having been more tired. It was the old plague of months of overscheduling and deafness to feelings and body. At that same time my brother on the East Coast, now a highly respected medical professor, was in the hospital recovering from what had appeared to be a heart attack but may have been the physiological complications of exhaustion. One day in the middle of the group process at Esalen I broke down. Sobbing grief and angry curses came out of me in a way that utterly surprised and frightened me. The issue was my father, now dead for over twenty-four years. We had never said goodbye. And I had never fully grieved, for "big boys don't cry." Nor could I remember when he had held me in his arms. Nor could I remember his ever telling me that he loved me. And now, like the playback of an old film, history seemed to be repeating itself in a way that I simply could not bear. Dad had worked himself to death prematurely, and now look at his sons. His genuine affection for us went largely unexpressed. Now my son Steve was a young man, about the age I was when my father died, and I could not remember the last time I had held him in my arms or told him that I loved him. That day at Esalen marked the beginning of another chapter of my journey.

Three years later a very special friend died. We had been good friends since seminary days. Our children had grown up together, we had helped each other with improvements at our summer cabins, and we were members of the same seminary faculty. In the seven months from the diagnosis of his cancer until his death, I learned a good bit more about male socialization and men's lives. Though we thought we had been close friends before, we had largely missed the experience of genuine vulnerability to each other. It took a terminal illness to bring that about. We prayed together, cursed together, laughed together, and cried together. In a sense it was all new. We shared our doubts, fears, and secrets in ways we had never done before. Thus, those months of hell were also months of incredible grace. But, sadly, it took a terminal illness to usher in that grace.

Within a few months of his death, I called six other male friends and told each of them my need for a men's support group. The response from each was virtually identical: "Jim, you know the kind of schedule I've got, and the last thing I need is another meeting. But count me in. I know I need this, too, and I'll put it high in my priorities." Today the group is still going strong, and for these several years has been a significant part of my own journeying.

One last vignette to my story. Not long ago an invitation came to preach in the chapel of a distinguished midwestern college. I had preached there before, but this invitation was different. This time the request had not come to me but to Wilys Claire. After years of homemaking and demanding volunteer work in church and community, she had begun a second career—entering seminary, graduating, taking additional clinical work, becoming ordained—and now was a hospital chaplain. It was she who was invited to preach. So this time it was I who went along as the supportive, dutiful spouse. It was I who sat in the second pew from the front and smiled encouragingly during the service. It was I who after chapel went to a luncheon in her honor and sat in the corner, observing that the students directed all their questions to her and none to me. At one level I found this enormously exciting. At another level I wondered how it would feel if I had no place of my own in the sun.

Enough for the pieces of my story. What does it all mean? The costs of male sexism are enormous. Certainly, women bear the brunt of those costs. It is women who have been forced into derivative identities. It is women who continue to experience subjugation in myriad interpersonal and institutional ways. What men have suffered cannot appropriately or fairly be compared.

Nevertheless, we men have experienced deprivation by our own doing and that of our forefathers. We who are male have lost touch with our vulnerability, our deepest human capacities for tenderness, our need for dependence—in short, a whole range of emotions. We simply don't feel very well. We are more alienated from our bodily existence, and our sexuality, instead of being a richly diffused sensuousness and invitation to intimacy, has

46

taken a narrow, genital focus. We lose touch with the concrete particularity of pulsing life and instead are seduced by abstractions, confusing them with reality. We seem to live with a constant need to prove self-worth through achievement and winning. We relate competitively with other men and find it easier to have buddies than deep friendships. Predictably, we males will die younger than women—about seven years at latest count. Gay men frequently break through the constrictions of the macho mold, but they suffer more oppression than lesbians because of the dynamics of male homophobia in our society. And our social institutions are tragically distorted by the exploitive, competitive, dominance-and-submission, violent aspects of traditional masculinism.[3]

What is the root of the problem? Why is the movement toward wholeness and equality so difficult? Why do human beings continue to live out those ancient dualisms of spirit-over-body and man-over-woman, dualisms that conjoined as men identified themselves with mind and spirit while labeling women as body and emotion? Why is it all so persistent and difficult to change? Consider six possibilities, each probably bearing some truth, all doubtlessly interrelated.

1. There is historical inheritance and conditioning. This is the way both sexes were brought up. We were simply reared to believe that men were superior and women inferior, to believe that men had one kind of mental and emotional nature and women another. And such was the Christian religious heritage, whether in the patriarchy of ancient Israel, or in Paul's reflection of the sexist mores of his day, or in the misogyny of Tertullian and Aquinas or that of Luther and Calvin.

Was this my personal heritage? Indeed, it was, even though I was not aware of its particulars for many years. I did grow up knowing that men had the responsibility and the destiny to rule. I did grow up knowing that men were to be in control of themselves as well as in control of women and all else. When I later read such chapters in the Christian story, I knew that I had learned my lesson well, long before understanding the historical details.

2. Related to the Christian heritage is the matter of biological misinformation. For centuries in a prescientific and patriarchal society it was believed that the male semen was the sole bearer of life. The woman was simply the ground into which the seed was planted. She provided the incubating space for life transmitted by the male. Indeed, it was not until 1827 that Western science knew anything about eggs and ovulation.

While I do not recall any specific knowledge of this mistaken biological theory (which curiously has a lingering effect), I do remember as part of the little sex education received from my father the admonition that I was always to guard my male powers. The life force was very precious and to be used only in marriage. I was impressed that somehow I as a male "possessed" it.

3. Another theory has to do with direct sexual fears. In Freudian psychology the notion of castration anxiety is commonplace. In order successfully to complete heterosexual intercourse, the penis must enter the vagina, and Freud theorized that this engulfing of the male organ could give rise to unconscious anxieties about its loss. The male then copes with such anxiety by transforming it into aggression against the female partner.

I have difficulty recognizing this anxiety as my experience. Yet some reflection on that hypothesis leads me to another application. The aggression is not so much an expression of castration anxiety as of performance anxiety. With this I can identify. For successful intercourse to take place I must perform. I must have an erection. There is always the threat of impotence, whether I have ever experienced it or not. But this can become symbolic of life beyond the direct sexual experience. Throughout my life, I have learned to perform. The penile erection can become symbolic of a whole way of life for one conditioned in the masculine mode. And a performance mode of life is not only demanding but also threatening. The fear of failure is always lurking in the wings. Then comes the temptation to express hostility toward those making the performance demands. If my genital performance is a central symbol of a whole way of life, I just might be angry at my partner and at women in general, for are they not requiring me to perform and threatening me with loss of esteem if I do not?

4. There is the possibility that sexism persists because of male envy of women's biological powers. Freud postulated that penis envy was common among women, a natural envy of the powerful and treasured male organ. Revisionist Freudian psychologists and feminists alike have strongly challenged this notion. There is no literal penis envy. Rather it is a resentment of dominant male power as such. (In fact, about the only place there is penis envy is in the men's locker room, where males themselves make surreptitious comparisons.) The real issue with which men must cope is womb envy. In spite of centuries of mistaken biological information about conception, men have always recognized that in the birthing process women are much more intimately involved with the generation of new life. It is an awesome, mysterious, powerful event in terms of which males seem to have a negligible role. Hence, we men have found ways of symbolizing and acting out our own capacities to give birth. Male-oriented scripture thus suggests that Adam gave birth to Eve. And the Father God

gave birth to the Son God. And male clergy resist sharing their powers of birthing new spiritual life at the baptismal font.

Does womb envy apply to me? Perhaps in ways I dimly recognize or am loath to admit. I do believe women are closer to the source and the newness of life. I do believe that women feel life more keenly and immediately, and I may well be inclined to envy and to punish them for what I lack.

5. A theory concerning the dynamics of male sexism speaks of "father-wounded sons." Cultural and religious mythology provides numerous examples of sons fearing the wounding power of their fathers. In Greek mythology there is Oedipus threatened by his father, Laius, and Oedipus fleeing to his mother to escape the wrath of his father. In the Old Testament there is Abraham, ready to sacrifice his son, Isaac, out of presumed obedience to God. In Christian history there are atonement theories (dreadfully misleading and yet still abounding in much popular theology) announcing that the Son must die to appease the wrath of the righteous Father.

How is the threat of father to son involved in misogyny? Consider how male children are typically reared in this society. By far the strongest identification in the first years of life is with the mother. She is present to the little boy while the father is absent. She is the warm, caring source of life and protection. But around the age of five or six boys are typically subjected to insistent and forceful demands from the father to renounce feminine and baby ways. Now it is time to become a man. (At about the age of three I had a treasured doll. When a year or so later the doll's head broke in two, I received messages that there would be no replacement. Now it was time for other things, sandlot football and the like. It was time to do real "boy things," i.e., manly things.) But what happens in this transitional period? I am called upon to trade the seemingly unconditional love of my mother for my father's world. While this other world bears promises of power and privilege, it carries the threat of many wounds. Everything now is conditional. My father's approval is conditional upon my performance. This is a world where I must compete with and ultimately be judged by other males, men who like my father always have the capacity to withhold their approval and to wound when achievement is not realized.[4]

6. Yet another possibility is homophobia, that irrational and unreasonable fear of same-sex attraction and affection. The dynamics are complex and many-sided. Ours is a particularly homophobic society, and women as well as men are marked by such fears. But clearly the stronger ones are directed by males toward male homosexuality. Consider two possible reasons.

The gay male threatens other males because he embodies the symbol of woman. Stereotypically it is assumed that in gay male sexual intercourse one of the partners must be passive and take the woman's role. But the assumption that a man would willingly submit to "womanization" can be a symbolic threat to every other male, regardless of his sexual orientation. The gay male threatens me with "womanization" in another way. I know that he has the capacity to view me not primarily as a person, but rather as a sex object, a desired body. But this is how straight men have so frequently viewed women. Hence, the gay man by his very being (quite apart from overt act) reminds me of the general male objectification of women and poses a psychic threat to treat me like one of them. Nor does the power of these dynamics depend upon one's conscious awareness of their presence.

There is still another dynamic that connects homophobia and male sexism.[5] It appears to be a constant of human nature that everyone needs validation and affection from his or her equals. But in a sexist society, those men who perpetuate and embrace male dominance have only men as their equals. Women are inferior. To seek validation, love, and affection from other men, however, is a fearful thing, for men have been taught to relate to other men on a different basis: competitiveness. The gay male who expresses affection toward other males symbolizes what seems denied to the rest of us. Hence, it is the gay male who receives the response of rage and oppression for having and for symbolizing that which other men lack and cannot have. Male homophobia injects distance into the relationships of father and son, of brother and brother, of men and men. As a consequence, men lean principally upon women for their validation and affection, and in so doing resent those very women precisely because they are not men's equals, and hence cannot adequately give what they have been asked to give.

If these are some of the dynamics that fuel the fires of continuing male sexism, what is at stake for both men and women in finding release from them?

There is an enormous amount at stake for each of us personally. For women, obviously, the promise is less oppression, greater justice, and fuller personhood. For men there is also a many-dimensioned promise, as I have tried to suggest in these pages.

For the church there is at stake a basic faithfulness to the gospel, a faithfulness to the fresh winds of the Spirit and to the great vision that in Christ there is neither Jew nor Greek, neither slave nor free, neither male nor female. At stake for the church is the issue of faithful theology. Such a task is never done, and the retheologizing of our language and imagery in sexually inclusive ways is a fundamental challenge of our day. At stake is a wholistic spirituality, for a masculinist-shaped spirituality will only perpetuate alienation.

At stake in the church is our leadership styles, which are still marked by hierarchy, achievement, and competition. Christians need to learn better how to equip "the saints" for the work of ministry. At stake is our worship, for we are still dominated by the rational, the cognitive, and the appeal to the mind and the ear. But there is a hunger for more wholistic worship wherein the experience of body and feeling and color and engagement of the whole person is caught up in responsiveness to the presence of God.

There is much at stake for the world, for a masculinist-dominated institutional structure and social policy has led humanity to the brink of disaster in its patterns of violence, racism, and ecological abuse, all intimately linked with the problem of patriarchy.

Theologically, the answer is not new, but I need to hear it again and again (just as the old gospel song puts it, "Tell me the old, old story, for I forget so soon"). The old story, forever new, has to do with the grace of God. It is a grace that says "You are accepted." Against all my works of the law, against all my anxious striving for achievement, control, dominance, winning, and proving my worth, there is a word of grace, a word that still becomes flesh. This kind of love casts out fear, and fear is the root of male sexism.

Of what am I afraid? Am I afraid of the awesome demands of my father and of my Father God? If so, I need to experience that gospel wherein the father runs out to meet the returning son. And I need to realize the gospel's paradox that my Father God is at the same time my Mother God who nurses humanity at her full breasts.

Am I afraid of losing in competition? Am I so committed to a competitive way of life that I live in constant fear? If so, there is a paradox in the gospel about losing life and finding life, and I need to hear that freshly.

Am I afraid of performance failure, whether sexually, professionally, or socially? If so, I need to understand anew that central paradox of the gospel that nothing I do earns the love of God. My worth is given.

Am I afraid of my negative emotions, particularly my anger? If so there is that gospel paradox which says that it is possible to be angry without sinning or alienating.

Am I afraid of losing my power and control? If so, there is that paradoxical figure who counted equality with God not a thing to be grasped, but emptied himself. He is the one who washed the disciples' feet.

Am I afraid of losing my strong, masculine, hetero-sexual self-image? Am I afraid of vulnerability and inti-macy? If so, I need to look again at that man who wept, who embraced the beloved disciple, who called out to others in his time of need.

Am I afraid of the child within me, afraid of the need for play, spontaneity, and feeling? If so, I need to hear again freshly Jesus' reminder that unless I turn and be-come like a little child I will not enter the New Age.

The issue of sex-role liberation is an issue for men as well as for women. It is not a passing fad. Nor is it some-thing trivial or simply a luxury for the comfortable and affluent. Nor is it just another cause for a few self-appointed crusaders. Rather, it is the issue with the most far-reaching implications for the church since the Refor-mation. And human survival just might have something to do with embracing this lost alternative.

Both women and men suffer under sexism. Both women and men yearn for liberation. That women have borne and continue to bear the brunt of oppression, there is no doubt. That men have had and continue to have the dominant power, there is no denying. But when men and women journey into this issue together, both personally and institutionally, we will all change. Then we might learn (in Tolstoy's words) to live more magnificently in this world.

· 4 ·

Sexuality Issues
in American Judaism
and Roman Catholicism

*D*uring the past decade there has been more focused attention given to sexuality issues in American religious life than perhaps ever before in our history. No previous period saw a comparable outpouring of books and articles. No previous decade produced as many ecclesiastical studies, debates, and pronouncements. No earlier time witnessed the emergence of so many caucuses and movements bent either on reforming the sexual views of the religious group in question or on protecting it from unwanted change.

My purpose in this chapter is to provide a brief overview of the general sexuality directions in Judaism and Roman Catholicism, giving special attention to two areas of particular development: women's issues and homosexuality. In chapter 5, I will examine Protestantism and sexuality issues. To this latter faith group I will give more detailed attention, for it is the group I know best.

The Situation in American Judaism

As in major Christian faith groups so also in Judaism there is a considerable spectrum of conviction on sexuality issues.[1] This spectrum falls roughly into denominational patterns, with Orthodox Judaism on the conservative end of the spectrum, Reform Judaism toward the liberal end, and Conservative Judaism somewhere in the middle.

Jews are united in affirming sexuality as a good gift from God and in emphasizing its linkage with stable family life. Compared to Christian traditions, Judaism has had less of an antisexual emphasis or a soul-body dichotomy. Marriage is typically seen as the only appropriate context for genital sexuality, and all sexual expressions except for marital genital coition have traditionally been condemned. Since Orthodox Judaism claims to be in possession of unchanging, correct dogma, and since it believes that nothing new can be added to Jewish theology or moral law, there has predictably been little discernable change in recent years in this branch. Contemporary changes in sexual mores are viewed by Orthodox Jews quite simply as loss of individual control and self-mastery.

In Jewish law and practice generally, the woman has been seen as a peripheral Jew. Though honored as wife and mother, she is excluded from the central symbol of faith, circumcision. In Orthodoxy, this understanding of her nature as secondary, derivative, and incomplete persists, even though it is acknowledged that a man without a woman is not completely human. Nevertheless, within Orthodoxy there is unrest, coming particularly from well-educated women who find their exclusion from the full religious life of the community highly questionable not only for women themselves but also for the status of Judaism.

In Conservative and especially in Reform Judaism, however, there is considerable change. Here Jewish feminists have tried to remain loyal to the tradition while emphasizing themes that allow for change. Thus the transcendence of God, the idea of covenant, and the theme of liberation become vehicles for liberation and inclusion rather than subordination and exclusion. If God is transcendent, female God-language is possible, for God is as much (and as little) female as male. If a personal God is to be retained, and if Jewish liturgy is not to make an idol of maleness, then feminine pronouns, images, and metaphors must be used. Some Jewish feminists have published sabbath prayers for women using only female imagery as well as distinctive ceremonies to celebrate the birth of Jewish daughters. Indeed, the self-liberation of Jewish women is seen by many feminists as intrinsic to the redemption of the Jewish people, whose heritage is born out of a liberation movement.[2]

At present, the question of the ordination of women results in varied answers. Orthodoxy refuses to consider the possibility, while in Conservative Judaism the issue is under official debate. Reform Judaism, however, affirms women's ordination, and increasingly female rabbis are finding acceptance within congregations, though most frequently as assistants or associates to senior male clergy.

Regarding homosexuality, Orthodoxy remains rigorously opposed. Homosexual orientation as well as its expression is seen as unbiblical, contrary to God's created order, and threatening to the solidity and sanctity of the family. But among Conservative and Reform Jews this strictly legal and repressive attitude is being modified by those who, citing certain scientific views, see homosexuality not as willful sin against God so much as pathology. Within Reform Judaism the greatest movement on the question has occurred. For theologians in this communion, the question is not so much whether one is a homosexual, but whether that person is willing to cast his or her lot fully with the religious community. While it may be too early to predict that Reform Judaism is moving toward acceptance of homosexuality as a life-style, there are some signs of such movement. Indeed, the first gay synagogue was established early in the 1970s and aligned

itself with Reform Judaism. Yet the majority of Conservative and Reform Jews are probably not willing either to
condemn gay males and lesbians uncompassionately or to
give them approval. Rather, they call for understanding
without normative approval and for protection of the civil
rights of homosexual people.

On other issues such as divorce, abortion, adultery,
and masturbation there seems to be a fairly consistent pattern. Orthodoxy retains an unwaveringly strict biblical-
legal attitude condemning these practices. Reform Jews
are more flexible, attending to varied circumstances, motivations, and meanings of such actions. Conservative Jews
fall somewhere in between.

The Roman Catholic Situation

While, unlike Jews (and Protestants), Roman Catholics are not divided into different denominations, it would
be patently false to conclude that there is a uniform viewpoint on sexual theology and ethics. The spectrum of conviction is wide here too.[3]

The position that for centuries dominated Vatican
teaching (and in which the majority of Roman Catholic
people have been educated) viewed the natural purpose
or end of sexual expression to be procreation and saw
sexual ethics governed by natural law, knowable through
human reason. The unitive or relational purpose of sexuality was also recognized but was considered secondary to
the primary purpose of procreation, which included not
only the producing of offspring but also their nurture and
education. With this natural-law basis it was possible to
derive clear moral judgments about a variety of sexual
acts. If the primary and natural purpose of sexual expression was procreative, then masturbation, homosexual intercourse, bestiality, and artificial birth control were all
forbidden, because each of these in its own way violates

the natural order. While fornication, adultery, incest, and rape do not violate the natural order (that is, they can all be expressions of heterosexual coition), they were nevertheless unjust because they deny the education of offspring.

This traditional view has been criticized on a variety of counts in recent years. Its rigid natural law, argue such theologians as Charles Curran and Philip Keene, is based on a static, nonhistorical view of the person. It judges morality solely in terms of the physical contours of actions rather than their relational meanings to persons. It is legalistic and tends to view sexual sins always as "grave" matters, giving them a weight that is unrealistic and unbiblical. Finally, it focuses disproportionately on genital sexuality.[4]

This view began to receive some ecclesiastical endorsement with Vatican Council II and its document *The Church in the Modern World* (1965). Here the unitive or relational meanings of sexuality were given prominence as well as the procreative. While the Catholic Church in its official teaching has not consistently embraced the Vatican II directions since that time, a number of the church's theologians have, and have pressed the analysis of sexuality further into a central focus on the dignity and wholeness of the person in his or her relationships. The most thoroughgoing expression of this newer approach appeared in the volume *Human Sexuality: New Directions in American Catholic Thought*.[5] Authored by a team of five Catholic scholars headed by Fr. Anthony Kosnick, this book was commissioned (though not officially approved) by the Catholic Theological Society of America. Hence it has occasioned serious debate within American Catholicism.

The Kosnick volume reflects a major shift. Now the focus is unequivocally on the person and his or her "creative growth toward integration"—not on procreation, natural law, or the physical contours of sexual acts. Seven values are singled out as particularly significant, characterizing actions that promote such growth and integration: the sexual expression will be self-liberating, other-enriching, honest, faithful, socially responsible, life-serving, and joyous. Central to these values is the gospel's law of love.

Obviously, this approach (and similar approaches by other Roman Catholic ethicists) cannot produce a neat catalogue of approved and disapproved sexual acts, as did the traditional view. It does suggest directions, however. While heterosexual marriage is clearly considered the ideal context for sexual intercourse, these theologians refuse to judge that every genital act outside of marital intercourse is intrinsically immoral. If variant patterns of extramarital relations are usually destructive of fidelity, it cannot be said with certainty that they are always so. Masturbation is no longer seen as unnatural and "seriously disordered," but rather as an act that can have many meanings, some of which may be justifiable.

While this reinterpretation of sexual ethics has found a warm reception in many quarters, it has occasioned considerable debate among Catholic moral theologians. It has been criticized for tentativeness and subjectivism in its judgments about specific sexual acts. It has been criticized on the grounds that its major norm of "creative growth toward integration" and its seven value criteria for measuring sexual acts are too general: they could apply to any human actions and are not specifically enough related to the distinctive arena of sexuality. And it has been criticized for an excessively psychological and consequentialist ethical methodology—a methodology, it is charged, which can easily slip into the popular stance that anything is all right if nobody gets hurt.[6] Nevertheless, these "new directions" continue to find support from many laity and clergy who welcome the person-centered, antilegalist approach. It is time, these people say, for the Catholic Church to affirm a sexual ethic which recognizes that the well-being of persons is primary and that, given the immense complexity of human relations, sexual acts cannot be neatly catalogued as good or bad, right or wrong, according to the physical nature of the acts themselves.

The position of the Kosnick volume on homosexual acts is an important illustration of the difference between the newer view and the Catholic tradition. These authors refuse to label homosexual acts as intrinsically evil or as natural and good. Rather, while finding homosexual acts "essentially imperfect" compared with the heterosexual ideal, they are to be evaluated in terms of their relational meanings and can be morally responsible when in the context of a close, stable relationship. In actual practice, some Roman Catholic priests and nuns have pioneered in establishing supportive organizations within the church for gay men and lesbians (Dignity, established in 1968) and in inaugurating special ministries to the homosexual Catholic (New Ways Ministry, headquartered in Baltimore).

In contrast, the traditional Catholic view affirmed by the Vatican maintains that homosexual acts are intrinsically disordered and can in no case be approved.[7] Such acts lack an essential and indispensable finality in the objective moral order; they violate natural law, fly in the face of scriptural condemnation, and constitute a threat to the family. Nevertheless, the homosexual person is to be treated with pastoral sensitivity.

Regarding the position of women, the Roman Catholic situation is perhaps as diverse as that within Protestantism and Judaism. Whereas the official Roman Catholic position long assumed the ontological inferiority of women, it has now evolved to a stance that maintains the essential equality and complementarity of the sexes, as well as the different duties of spouses within marriage. The differences between men and women should be respected but never used to justify domination. While the church, acting in the social sphere, must defend the rights of women, their admission to the full priesthood is still forbidden.

But there are also reformist and radical Roman Catholic feminist movements. Reformist theologians such as Rosemary Ruether and Elisabeth Fiorenza have made systematic critiques of the dualistic and hierarchical mentality the church inherited from the classical world.[8] They have related the issues of masculinist God-language, the exclusion of women from church leadership, the teachings on marriage and family, and the pervasive sexism of the Roman Catholic tradition to an entire world view falsified by male ideology. Yet such Catholic feminists continue to claim their place within the church, believing that the core Christian affirmations are capable of being purged of their sexist dimensions. On the ecclesiastical level there has been, within recent years, a concerted campaign for the ordination of women priests. Other feminists, such as Mary Daly, however, have concluded that the Catholic, indeed, entire Christian tradition is itself irreformably sexist, and have moved outside the church to a "post-Christian" orientation.[9]

The issue of artificial contraception continues to plague the Catholic scene. The more liberal theologians insist that the difference between the rhythm method and artificial contraceptives is ethically insignificant. The morality or immorality of married sexual expression cannot be based upon such issues but rather upon the couple's relationship and their responsible parenting.[10] Conservative theologians, including Vatican teachings, insist, however, that artificial contraception is still an offense against the natural law. Public opinion surveys show that the significant majority of American Catholic couples in their own practice side with the liberal theologians on this issue and consider it a matter of personal conscience.

A Concluding Word

While Judaism and Roman Catholicism each exhibits its own unique understanding and history as it deals with sexuality issues, there are commonalities and differences that regularly cross the lines—as will be observed, also, in Protestantism. The Orthodox Jew and the traditional Roman Catholic may be worlds apart on some theological matters, but they will find each other amazingly compatible when it comes to sexuality and the family. Likewise, the liberal Catholic and the Reform Jew discover a strong mutual attraction on these issues, while at the same time differing vigorously with others within their own faith traditions.

To be sure, there are forces that strongly resist the changes mentioned in these pages. A current pope who is markedly conservative on sexuality issues and a Jewish tradition that continues to celebrate certain patriarchal patterns both portend resistance. Nevertheless, growing numbers in the mainstreams of each faith tradition insist that "the sabbath was made for persons, not persons for the sabbath" (see Mark 2:27)—that is, forms of sexual expression finally must be evaluated in accordance with genuine human fulfillment.

If there is one overriding theme that binds people of all major faith groups together regardless of their conservatism or liberalism, however, it is this: compared with the not-too-distant past, religiously concerned people now are much less likely to equate sexuality as such with sin. They are more likely to understand it as a divine gift—even if they continue to differ in their convictions regarding its appropriate expressions.

· 5 ·

Sexuality in Protestant
Interpretations

Sexuality in Protestantism is a fascinating and confusing picture.[1] While in Jewish and Roman Catholic traditions there are divergent views and emphases, within Protestantism this is multiplied manyfold. With an enormous denominational diversity, with the absence of a central ecclesiastical teaching authority, with differing convictions on biblical interpretation and on the weight to be given to contemporary sources, it is even more difficult to speak meaningfully of "a Protestant position" on sexuality than with the other major faith groups.

What Protestants Have in Common

Despite the divergences, there are several commonalities that might characterize the majority of Protestants. One is the affirmation that sexuality is a good gift of the Creator that has been marred and distorted by human sin. Our sexuality is a basic dimension of our humanness. It includes but is not limited to genital feelings and expression. Sexuality is our way of being in the world as male or

Original essay © 1983, University of Denver.

female persons, involving our varied and unique self-understandings of masculinity and femininity, our sexual-affectional orientations, our perceptions of our embodiedness, and our capacities for sensuousness and emotional depth. All this is God's good gift to human beings, God's way of drawing us out of isolation and into communication and communion. But Protestants believe that sexuality, like every other dimension of human life, has been marred and distorted by "the fall." Our alienation from God, from neighbor, and from ourselves is experienced sexually as well as in other ways.

A second commonality is that the two alienating dualisms regarding sexuality are part of all Protestant history. The first, spiritualistic or Hellenistic dualism, is shared with Roman Catholics. It is the body-spirit split that pervaded Greek philosophy and culture at the beginning of the Christian era. While the Jewish tradition is significantly free of spiritualistic dualism, it has been heavily marked by sexist or patriarchal dualism, and Christians—Roman Catholic and Protestant alike—share this distortion. The two dualisms came together as men assumed that the superior part (spirit, male) was destined to lead and discipline the inferior part (body, female).

The third Protestant commonality, in distinction from the Roman Catholic tradition, is the lack of a history that exalted virginity and celibacy as superior to married sexual life. This break with Catholicism came when the sixteenth-century Reformation theologically undercut salvation by good works (including virginity and celibacy) and, at the same time, elevated the doctrine of Christian marriage.

Fourth, Protestantism rather early abandoned procreation as the primary purpose of marriage and sexual expression. Instead of procreation, the fundamental aim became the expression of faithful love.

Fifth, mainstream Protestantism (as distinguished from ultraconservative and fundamentalist groups) has showed considerable openness in recent years to new empirical knowledge about sexuality, the historically and culturally relative nature of sexual norms, and feminist consciousness concerning the pervasive conditioning by male sexism of the church's understandings.

Finally, there has emerged within mainstream Protestantism the desire to move from an essentially negative approach to a more positive one, from a physically oriented focus on categories of sexual acts to a more interpersonal focus on the meanings of sexual expressions.

The Sixteenth Through Nineteenth Centuries

The Protestant Reformation of the sixteenth century brought with it some important shifts from the Catholic tradition on certain, if not all, sexuality issues. The two pervasive dualisms—spirit over body and man over woman—underwent important theoretical modifications, even though their tenacious hold continued in other ways.

Two doctrinal emphases of the Reformers were directed at spiritualistic dualism. First, they regarded as quite unbiblical the Catholic medieval distinction between the lower realm of nature and the higher realm of grace. The medievalists tended to see sex itself as inherently tainted and sinful, part of the lower realm of nature that must be transcended through the church's means of grace, even while the married couple was obligated to propagate the race. The Reformers could not view nature (and with it, sex) as in itself evil. Rather, the evil lay in the corruption of the human will and in the ways that fallen people expressed themselves in the natural (and sexual) realms.

The second doctrinal distinction was the Reformers' strong insistence on justification by grace rather than by works of the law. If no human achievement could merit divine favor, then there could be no special merit to sexual celibacy. The cult of virginity was thus undercut both by the affirmation of the essential goodness of nature and by the emphasis on salvation by grace. Marriage was lifted to a new level of Christian affirmation, and Martin Luther advised monks and nuns to abandon celibacy for the married state.

Nevertheless, the Protestant Reformers had considerable ambivalence about sexuality. Luther himself was both a radical and a conservative in this regard. On the one hand, he treated sex with an earthy frankness and honesty seldom seen in theological writings. He believed that in most persons (especially males) sexual desire had an urgency and compulsion that could not be denied. Hence, while God had ordained marriage as a great gift, a "school of heavenly love" for the spouses and their offspring, at the same time marriage was "a hospital for the sick," an emergency arrangement for the illness of human drives. In the fallen human being, sexuality was always pervaded by lust and corrupted. Yet God's strange work was to take a couple's corrupted sexual desire, and through pardon and permission make of it a vehicle for propagating the race and restraining human sin.

John Calvin was somewhat less pessimistic. If Luther's main concern was to confine the raging power of sex within marriage, Calvin believed that sex could have constructive effects for the couple, provided that there was mutual consent between the spouses and provided any sexual activity was moderate and within the appropriate bounds of "delicacy and propriety." If self-control and modesty were to characterize all sexual expression in marriage, then there followed an immediate gain for the wife's position. While Luther had believed that the sex instinct was felt so strongly by the husband that the wife must submit, it was not so with the Geneva Reformer. There must be mutual discipline and respect. If to Calvin the woman's status was still subordinate to the man's, still there was a notable development taking place. He began to believe that it was companionship rather than procreation and the restraint of lust that was God's chief design for marriage. This was to have major consequences for later Protestant thought.

Nevertheless, neither Reformer could break cleanly with certain medieval assumptions. If in theory sex was natural and not sinful, still in practice sexual acts were viewed with suspicion. Further, like their Christian predecessors, Luther and Calvin did not look upon sexuality as a fundamental dimension of human nature, but rather dealt more narrowly with sexual acts.[2]

While there was a chipping away at sexist dualism, particularly in the Calvinistic emphasis on companionship, the Reformation also resulted in some backward steps concerning sexual equality. In the Roman Catholic tradition, women had the church's blessing to live independently of men and to make their own contributions to the church through the female religious orders. Now, however, these orders were abolished for Protestants, and the housewifely ideal for women was given divine blessing. Further, the Protestant Reformers turned to the Old Testament patriarchs for models of what the Christian family should be. Even Calvin, who saw the woman more positively than did most earlier male theologians, saw her as the man's subordinate helper and support. In addition, certain ecclesiastical practices implicitly reinforced traditional masculinism. Reacting against serious churchly abuses, some notable Reformers such as Ulrich Zwingli attacked physical representations in churches—stained glass, crucifixes, images of the Virgin, even church organs. Such things were emotional and stirred up fleshly feelings, whereas "true worship" was disciplined and controlled. But the iconoclastic attack on the physical and the emotional was also a buttress to traditional male control over the so-called female impulses.[3]

The most significant Protestant developments in the two centuries following the Reformation took place among the heirs of Calvin: the Puritans, the Quakers, and some of the Anglicans. These groups developed an increasing conviction that procreation was not the major purpose of sexuality. Rather, love and companionship were. Thus, Richard Baxter could speak of mutual comfort and nurture as the chief end of sexuality, and his fellow Anglican Jeremy Taylor could speak of the value of sexual intercourse "to lighten and ease the cares and sadnesses of household affairs" and "to endear each other."[4] And the great English Puritan poet John Milton (in spite of his subordinationism regarding women) was convinced that the sexual union of spouses could prefigure the heavenly realm. Indeed, so convinced was Milton that companionship (not procreation) was the chief end of marriage that in his tract "The Doctrine and Discipline of Divorce" he made a brief for accepting divorce on the grounds of incompatibility, a remarkable departure from previous Christian teaching.

Contrary to some unfair stereotypes that have branded Puritans as simply sex-negative, the picture was not that simple. True, their emphasis on discipline led to frequent legalisms, and they were often harsh in punishment of fornication and adultery. Yet their writings concerning the positive joys and gifts of marital sex attest to the other side. In addition to the companionate over the procreative emphasis on sexuality, the Puritans were noteworthy for one other development: their understanding of marriage. For the sixteenth-century Reformers, the church's role in marriage was purely instrumental, pronouncing God's blessing upon a sexual union that was a matter primarily between the couple and God. With the

Puritans, however, the church's role increased. Now marriage became an act in which the church as a social institution gave its approval and permission to a couple to live in sexual covenant. The shift at this point was away from sexuality as a natural (if distorted) good of life and a shift toward a belief that sexuality itself was something that expressly required the church's approval for its exercise.

Nineteenth-century Protestantism on the whole provided few new developments in sexual understandings. In England and America, the century was largely marked by the Victorian retrogression: a strong suspicion of sexuality, including marital sexual excess, horror over masturbation and homosexuality, and the Comstock laws to erase sexual obscenity. Victorianism also brought with it a strong tendency toward "spiritual femininity"—the placing of women (especially of the middle and upper classes) on a pedestal, characterizing them as delicate and above the animality of sex. Thus, the Victorian mother's advice to her daughter for the latter's wedding night: "Just close your eyes, dear, and think of England." One other development in late nineteenth-century Protestantism, however, was different: the social justice emphasis. Both the women's suffrage and the Protestant Social Gospel movements lifted up women's rights as a major concern for church and society.

Twentieth-century Developments

Early twentieth-century American Protestantism was marked by an internal tension of values over the issue of contraception. Particularly in its first two decades, the exclusivistic vision of "a Protestant America" was still strong. This vision included a strong emphasis on the duty of Protestant families to procreate abundantly in order to stem the dilution of this religious dominance by the increasing waves of Catholic immigration. By the century's third decade, however, both the sinfulness and futility of this vision were largely recognized. Furthermore, Protestants, with their inveterate individualistic strain coupled with their openness to science and technology, became the religious supporters of individual procreative decisions and the use of contraception for family planning.

Toward the middle of this century, Protestant academic theology was moving decisively away from a law-centered and act-focused ethics and toward an attempt to base sexual morality more fully on interpersonal considerations. This shift went hand in hand with a new recognition that sexuality is a fundamental dimension of human life, an appreciation owed in no small measure to developments in modern psychology. The decades of the 1960s and 1970s saw Protestant theologians and church bodies attempting to respond to the rising movement of feminist women and gay men and lesbians, both outside and within the churches. The pluralism typical of Protestants on so many theological, ecclesiastical, and social issues became increasingly a fact of life in matters sexual.

To characterize current Protestant attitudes requires a distinction (a rough one but perhaps defensible) between Evangelicals and mainline denominations.[5] The former emphasize personal religious experience, conversion, evangelism, and the centrality of the Bible in doctrine and morals. Many of them remain highly traditional about sexual ethics, and yet two developments in Evangelical Protestantism are significant.

One development is the shift of numerous fundamentalist Evangelicals into right-wing political activism. The Moral Majority and similar groups of the New Right in religion and politics have centered considerable attention on sexuality issues, condemning homosexuality, pornography, abortion, and the Equal Rights Amendment, and exalting the male-dominated nuclear family as the normative family style and only valid sexual unit. Other paramount New Right concerns such as prayer in public schools, resistance to further racial integration, support of military superiority, and a politics of international confrontation may not, on first glance, appear to be sexual issues. Yet each suggests an ideology that is both highly masculinist and suspicious of sexuality.

Quite different are left-wing Evangelicals. Here the familiar emphases on personal religious experience and scriptural authority are mated with liberal, even radical, social justice concerns, including a fresh look at numerous sexuality issues. Feminist concerns are taken seriously. In contrast to the New Right's strident condemnation of homosexuality, left-wing Evangelicals support social justice for lesbians and gays, and exhibit some movement toward affirming the committed homosexual relationship as valid and analogous to heterosexual marriage.

Mainline denominational Protestantism shows considerable sexual ferment. Moving away from a dominant focus on rules and categories of actions, such Protestant sexual ethics now characteristically give greater attention to relationships, motivations, and concrete situations, convinced that ethics must be oriented fundamentally toward persons rather than toward abstract concepts. These emphases, together with an openness to clinical and social sciences, have led Protestants to reevaluate a variety of sexual expressions and to begin to rethink the meanings of sexuality.

A Constructive Statement

The following diagram suggests what I believe to be a slowly emerging paradigmatic shift in at least some Protestant (and other religious) thinking about sexuality.

From the Old Paradigm	To a New Paradigm
1. Theologies about human sexuality	1. Sexual theologies
2. Sexuality as either incidental to or detrimental to the divine-human relationship	2. Sexuality as intrinsic to the divine human relationship
3. Sin as essentially wrong sexual acts, violations of sexual norms	3. Sin as alienation from our divinely intended sexuality
4. Salvation as antithetical to sexuality	4. Salvation as including the recovery of sexual wholeness
5. Sexuality as incidental to the life of the church	5. Sexuality as fundamental to and pervasive in the life of the church

Some comment on each item is in order.

Sexual theology. The vast majority of religious statements on sexuality in the past have assumed essentially a one-way question: what does Christian theology (or the Bible, or the church's tradition) say about human sexuality? It is important now that we recognize another question as well. The clue comes from those Christians writing liberation theologies from feminist, black, and third-world perspectives. They are insisting that their own experience (in those instances, the experience of oppression) affords extraordinarily important insights into the meanings of Christian faith itself. Thus, for sexuality as well, the concern becomes two-directional, dialogical and not monological. In addition to the still-important question of what our religious tradition says about human sexuality is another question: What does our experience as sexual human beings say about the ways in which we experience God, interpret our religious tradition, and attempt to live the life of faith?

Sexuality and the divine-human relationship. How does God make the divine presence and meaning known and real to human life? Christian faith makes the bold claim

that the most decisive experience of God occurs not fundamentally or primarily in doctrine, creed, ideas, or in mystical, otherworldly experience. Rather, it happens in flesh.
"And the Word became flesh and dwelt among us, full of
grace and truth [John 1:14]." Christian faith is one of incarnation. And while Christians confess that they have seen
God with greatest clarity and focus in and through one
human being—Jesus, whom we call Christ—it is an error
to limit God's incarnation to that one figure, as decisive
and central as he is for the faith community. By limiting
God's incarnation to him alone we both deny his genuine
humanity and treat him as an anomalous exception to the
general human condition. Further, we close ourselves off
from the richness of the incarnationalist faith itself: the
realization that God continues to be experienced fundamentally in the embodied touching of human life with
human life. Our sexuality, in its full sense, is both the
physiological and the psychological grounding of our capacity to love. It expresses God's intention that we find
our authentic humanness not in isolation but in communion, an intention that applies equally to the genitally active and to the celibate, to the aged and to the youthful, to
the able-bodied and to the disabled.

Sexual sin. It has been commonplace in Christian
understanding to think of sexual sin in terms of certain
acts: sexual acts done with the wrong person, against divine or natural law, or harmful to others and the self.
While there is, indeed, truth in the assumption that sin
will be *expressed* in acts, it is a mistake to equate the two. In
its better moments theology has long known that sin basically is the experience and condition of alienation. And
alienation is inevitably experienced simultaneously in
three dimensions: alienation from God, from the neighbor, and from the self.

This is true of sexual sin. More basic than any particular acts, sexual sin is alienation from our divinely intended sexuality. It is experienced as alienation within and from the sexual self. The sexual body becomes object, either that which is to be constrained out of fear or that which is a pleasure machine but essentially other than the self. This is spiritualistic dualism. But it is also sexist dualism, for it is alienation from the neglected half of one's intended humanness, with males fearful of tenderness, emotion, and vulnerability, and females fearful of (or kept from) claiming their strength, assertiveness, and intellect.

Sexual sin is also sexual alienation from the neighbor. Emotions and bodies are distanced, and relationships are truncated. Sexual distortions contribute to dehumanizing uses of power and manipulation, to social violence, to persisting expressions of racism, and to ecological abuse. Sexual sin, most basically, is alienation from God. Thus in Christian history both spiritualistic and sexist dualisms helped mightily to shape the notion of a hierarchical, ladder type of spirituality. As one "progressed upward" in spirituality, one loved God quite apart from any creaturely love, and both neighbor and self became incidental to, if not inimical to, the love of God. The soul was envisioned as a solitary, uncontaminated virgin contemplating a similarly solitary and uncontaminated deity. But such spirituality cannot in the end nurture and express the intimate relationship of God, neighbor, and self, for it is inherently an invitation to division and distance.

Sexual salvation. Unfortunately, throughout the greater part of Christian history, spiritualistic dualism has so marked Christian thought and experience that salvation has been associated with disembodiment and release from the realm of the flesh into the "higher" life of the spirit. Yet, more authentic to the heart of both Christian and Jewish faiths is the claim that the experience of salvation in this life, incomplete though it may be, involves a greater realization of our sexual wholeness. If sin is basically alienation, salvation is reconciliation. If sexual sin is fundamentally alienation from divinely intended sexuality, sexual salvation involves reconciliation and reintegration of the sexual self. It is "resurrection of the body."

Two classic words from the Christian tradition deserve reinterpretation in this light. The process of salvation traditionally (and quite rightly) has been understood to involve the polar experiences of justification by grace and sanctification by grace. Justification refers to God's activity directed toward the self from "outside." It is the Cosmic Lover's radical, unconditional, unearned acceptance of the person. When one experiences this radical acceptance as directed toward the total body-self (and not toward some discarnate spirit), one begins to reclaim the lost sexual dimensions of the self. One's body feelings, one's fantasies, one's masculinity and femininity, one's heterosexuality and homosexuality, one's sexual irresponsibility as well as one's yearning for sexual integrity—all are graciously accepted by the divine Love. In the moment of that realization, everything is transformed. If the old fears, dualisms, and alienations return—as they will—still the self is not the same as before.

Sanctification, the second dynamic of salvation, refers to God's activity *within* the self. Traditionally, it has frequently been understood as growth toward a spiritualized, antibody, antisexual "holiness." More adequately, sanctification might be seen as God's gracious empowerment within, which both includes and enables the self's increasing sexual wholeness and fulfillment.

This might mean several things. It might mean growth in self-acceptance and positive self-love, the kind that "personalizes" the body, making me more vitally aware that I can celebrate the body which I am and thus affirm the ways in which my body-self relates to the world. Sanctification can mean growth in the capacity for

77

sensuousness, wherein the body becomes a means of grace and the graceful expression of the body a vehicle for love. It can mean renewal of the capacity for play. It can involve the diffusion of the erotic throughout the entire body rather than the narrow focus of sexual feeling in the genitals only. With such resexualization of the body might come an eroticization of the world, wherein our experienced environment reclaims the sensuous qualities that we had forgotten or failed to recognize. Sexual sanctification can mean growth in the possibility of androgyny, wherein each individual finds freedom to lay claim to his or her own unique personality configuration and expression and is not coerced into rigid sex-role stereotypes that make us half-human. Supremely, sexual sanctification means the awakening of the self to its destiny as an embodiment of love, the reintegration of our sexual dimensions around love's meanings.

If human experience of salvation is partial, incomplete, and fragmentary (as it is), surely this is true of the salvation that involves our sexuality. But its partiality does not negate its reality. The Word is made flesh, and our flesh is confirmed.

The church as a sexual community. Throughout most of Protestant history sexuality has been seen as incidental to the life of the church or even inimical to the church's purpose. It is time that this community of faith, worship, and service be understood also as a sexual community, not only because its members are sexual beings, but also because sexual meanings and feelings pervade all dimensions of the community's life, both for good and for ill. This has always been the case, and its conscious recognition can assist the church to reform the distorted sexual aspects of its life.

The church is a sexual community in its theological expressions, as the feminist movement forcefully reminds us. Stereotypically masculine language and images have pervaded Christian understandings of God and hence have given rise to a masculinized spirituality. A more androgynous theology and language can nuture a more androgynous spirituality, and both will be truer to the best in the tradition.

Reclaiming positive dimensions of sexuality in liturgy and sacramental life can enhance the connections of those experiences with the lives of the worshipers. Mainline Protestant worship has been marked, on the whole, by a masculinized emphasis on the spoken word and a suspicion of body feelings—touch, movement, color, play, and imagination. To the extent that worship patterns reflect the alienating sexual dualisms, they reinforce those dualisms in the lives of the worshipers. Further, recapturing an awareness of the rich sexual imagery in the two Protestant sacraments—baptism (the womb of new birth) and the Lord's Supper ("This is my body, given for you")— might assist the participants' understanding of the ways in which the total human sexual experience itself has sacramental potentialities. Sexual love, at its best, does have the capacity to break the self open not only to deep communion with the partner but also to the life-giving communion with God.

In education and social witness, consciousness of the church as sexual community can also expand our Christian awareness. Beyond the neglected but important role of the church in positive and effective sexuality education for its members of all ages, there can arise sensitivity to the sexual dimensions of a vast variety of social justice issues that the church is called to address. Some justice issues are quite obviously sexual: justice for women, gays, and lesbians; abortion; sexual abuse of women and children; prostitution; pornography; family planning and population control, to mention just a few. Beyond these are even larger social issues that do not appear to be sexuality-related, but in fact are. Patterns of distorted sexuality contribute enormously to social violence and militarism, to stubbornly persisting white racism, to the ecological dilemma and abuse of the natural environment. When the church can more fully realize the ways in which it is also a sexual community, when it can affirm more celebratively the potential sacramentality of human sexuality, then it may also more fully grasp the vision of an erotic sensibility toward the whole human community in a sacramental world.

Foundations for a Protestant Sexual Ethic

While there are different nuances and emphases within Roman Catholic sexual ethics, that presence of a strong natural-law tradition within that communion together with a clearly defined teaching authority, the *magesterium*, has resulted in a more coherent body of teachings than is true for Protestants. Protestantism has largely attempted to formulate sexual ethics from biblical grounds. The resultant ethics show a considerably greater variety, coming as they do from a diversity of faith communities with looser patterns of authority in doctrine and morals.

Historically, Catholic ethics have their strengths, particularly in universality of application, objectivity of norms, and in the attempt to be specific in application. But those strengths have been matched by certain weaknesses: a rigid insistence upon absolute moral judgments about specific acts and a strong tendency to evaluate sexual acts in terms of their physical contours.

Protestant sexual ethics have been strong in their attempt to be faithful to scriptural sources, in their openness to change, uniqueness, and particularity, and in their attempt to take motives and dispositions as seriously as the physical acts themselves. But Protestant ethics perennially have had difficulty in finding a firm grounding for sexual values and norms, and in finding ways of adjudicating conflicting norms. Protestants, moreover, have been less clear methodologically. Attempting to affirm the Bible as primary authority within a plurality of other sources, mainstream Protestants have discovered that the relativity of biblical texts and themes has made it difficult to specify particular rules of sexual conduct and to demonstrate the primacy of the Bible's authority.[6]

Protestant ethics have thus struggled to find a course between legalism on one side and normlessness on the other. Legalism is the attempt to apply precise laws and rules to actions regardless of the unique features of the context of those actions. It assumes that objective standards can be applied in the same way to whole classes of actions without regard to the particular meanings those actions have to particular persons. And it might be noted that the tendency toward legalism seems stronger in sexual morality than in virtually any other arena of human behavior.

The antidote to legalism is an ethics that finds its center and direction in *love* rather than in a series of specific, absolute injunctions. Such an ethics takes the Bible seriously, but understands the need for critical awareness of how its sexual teachings and practices not only reflect the biblical community's perception of God's intentions but also reflect sexual mores common to those historical circumstances. A love-centered ethics understands human nature as grounded in the will to communion. We are thoroughly social beings, nurtured into our humanness in community and destined for ultimate communion. This means that the positive ethical claim upon us is to become what we essentially *are*. We are to realize through our actions a responsiveness to the divine loving. Negatively, sin is not fundamentally breaking moral codes or disobeying moral laws (though it may involve that). More basically, sin is the failure to become who we are, the failure of our responsiveness to the Cosmic Lover. Sin is the estrangement and alienation that distort fulfillment and destroy communion.

Our sexuality is a dramatic sign of our destiny to communion, for its dynamism presses us toward intimacy and community. Even its distortions witness negatively to the power of sexuality by oppressing and destroying persons and their fulfillment.

If love is the central (albeit not the only) norm for Christian ethics, it is the central meaning of human sexuality and the measuring standard and justification for any particular sex act. Nevertheless, the word is dangerously slippery, and countless dehumanizing acts have been done in the name of love.

Love's source is God, the Creator, Redeemer, and Sustainer. Love takes its content from the Christian community's historic perceptions, both in scripture and tradition, of God's ways with humankind. Sexual acts that respond to the loving of God will be marked by qualities which mirror and reflect God's own creativity, reconciling activity, and sustaining, fulfilling purposes.

Love is multidimensional. Christian ethics long has utilized the four classic distinctions in speaking of love: epithymia or libido (the desire for sexual fulfillment); eros (desire and aspiration for the beloved); philia (mutuality and friendship); and agape (freely offered self-giving). These are different dimensions of love's unity, not different or opposing kinds of love. Each needs the other. Thus sexual desire (epithymia), without the desire for communion with and fulfillment in the other (eros), without a strong element of mutuality and friendship (philia), and without the transformative quality of self-giving abandonment (agape), becomes distorted.

Love is also indivisible and nonquantifiable in regard to other-love and self-love. Self-love has been a perennial problem in Protestant ethics, and the confusion here has spawned enormous sexual confusions. Self-love has been mistakenly confused with egocentrism and selfishness, hence condemned. Thus Protestantism has had a difficult time dealing positively with sexual pleasure in general and with certain issues such as masturbation in particular. Without positive self-love, however, authentic intimacy is impossible, for the possibility of intimacy rests in considerable measure upon each individual's own sense of worth as a person. Without such self-affirmation, we elevate the other person into the center of our lives, hoping that the partner will assure us of our own reality. But that is too large an order for the other; it idolizes the partner. Self-love and other-love are not antagonists, but are mutually complementary.

Furthermore, love expresses itself in a variety of values. These can become criteria by which specific sexual acts might be measured in a nonlegalistic manner (and here I draw upon the group of Roman Catholic scholars mentioned in chapter 4).[7] Love is self-liberating. In a sexual act, it expresses one's own authentic self-affirmation and also the desire for further growth. Love is also other-enriching, displaying a genuine concern for the well-being and growth of the partner. Sexual love is honest, expressing as truthfully as possible the meaning of the relationship that actually exists between the partners. Love is faithful, expressing an ongoing commitment to this relationship, yet without crippling possessiveness. Sexual love is socially responsible, concerned that sexual acts reflect values which enhance the larger community. Love is life-serving; the power of renewed life is shared by the partners when sexual expression has been appropriate. Authentic sexual love is joyous, exuberant in its appreciation of love's mystery, life's gift, and sex's playfulness.

Does such a perception of love involve any principles and rules for sexual ethics? Yes, it can give structure to ethics without the rigidities of legalistic absolutes. It can provide general principles. For example, love presses us toward a single and not a double standard for sexual morality. The same considerations apply equally to male and female, aged and young, able-bodied and disabled, homosexual and heterosexual. Another of love's principles is that the physical expression of one's sexuality with another person ought to be appropriate to the level of shared commitment. Such principles as these do not give exact prescriptions about specific acts, but rather provide a direction for making such decisions.

An ethics centered in love can also have specific sexual rules. It will probably understand the authority of the rules, however, in a certain way. Such rules are not likely to be understood as exceptionless absolutes (a new invitation to legalism). Nor will they be understood simply as guidelines that can be dismissed lightly if they do not seem to fit. Rather, love's sexual rules will have weight without absolutism. They will express the wisdom of the moral community and serve as a check on human finitude and sin, our limitations in both knowledge and virtue. People will take such prima facie rules seriously and presume in their favor. But given the rich complexity of human situations and God's freedom to intend the new expression of love, these moral rules will not be exceptionless. Yet, the community having presumed in favor of the rules, the burden of proof is upon the one who would depart from them. Now the question is: given a particular situation, will an exception to the rule actually express greater loyalty to the divine loving experienced in the neighbor, in the self, and in the wider community?

An ethics centered in this kind of love will be neither legalistic nor antinomian. It will not guarantee freedom from mistakes in the sexual life. It will place considerable responsibility upon the individual. It will be sensitive to relationships, motivations, and concrete situations, and it will be more oriented toward persons than toward abstract concepts. It will be more concerned about the authentic fulfillment of persons than the stringencies of unyielding laws or the neat cataloguing of types of sexual acts. It can serve our human becoming and our maturation as lovers in the image of the Cosmic Lover by whom and in whom we are continually being created.

Some Specific Sexual Issues

Marriage, family, and divorce. Protestantism early elevated the institution of marriage by rejecting meritorious celibacy and insisting that marriage was one of God's natural orders, an order of creation. Especially in the Puritan experience, the family was viewed as an indispensable moral unit of society and as the church's crucial subcommunity for Christian nurture. For all the religious attention given to the family by the church, however, several theological problems have persisted.

One has been the overly sharp distinction between nature and grace, between marriage as an order of creation and marriage as a sacrament or order of redemption. Protestantism early insisted upon the former, holding marriage to be a worldly and not a sacramental institution. It has no redemptive significance. No one is saved through it. God has established it, and its validity does not depend on the church's rites or on the couple's faith. All this has distinguished Protestant from prevailing Roman Catholic views. This view of marriage, however, tends to establish a sharp disjunction between nature and grace, a dualism of lower and higher orders that undercuts a fully incarnationalist theology wherein we might see that the whole creation and its embodied, fleshly relationships are potential media of God's healing and life-giving salvation.

Protestants sensed (appropriately, I believe) the unwarranted imperialism of the medieval church's claim that marriage was an official sacrament, which implied that only those whom the church officially blessed were truly married. Protestants appropriately insisted that it was the covenant of the two parties that was crucial. The covenant was blessed by God and the church, to be sure, but it was the covenant that was primary. Protestant theology has less adequately expressed the manner in which marriage can have sacramental and redemptive qualities. It is not the only human relationship through which the healing and humanizing love of God can be vividly encountered, but surely it is a primary arena for many people. Among Protestants, perhaps Anglicans have more fully recognized this than most others.[8]

Another Protestant problem is its tendency to interpret the notion of "co-humanity" in a way that makes heterosexual marriage the only means through which persons can truly recognize their divinely intended humanity. What theologians have wanted to affirm is that the "image of God" is not something possessed by the solitary individual. Rather, we are created as relational beings, destined for communion, whose sexuality is intrinsic and not peripheral to our capacity for co-humanity. This admirable emphasis, however, has frequently led to two major problems.

One is the suggestion that fully human existence is possible only in marriage—an imperious claim that unfairly leaves the permanently single, the separated and divorced, the widowed, and the gay or lesbian person in a second-class human status. In fact, Jesus himself would not qualify for full humanity. It is far better to say that we are created for communion and relationship, and that heterosexual marriage is *one* important form through which this might be realized.

A related issue is the tendency of some Protestant theologians to give certain sex-role characteristics an ontological status, overlooking both their historical relativity and the dehumanizing features of many masculine and feminine images. If I assume that as a man I am incomplete without a woman because I am by nature cognitive and she by nature intuitive, I strong and assertive, she vulnerable and nurturing, and because of these differences the two halves need each other to make one whole, then we have a marriage built on truncated and alienating sex-role assumptions. It is far better to insist that marriage is not the union of the two "natures" but of two unique persons, a personal relationship whose meaning is love.[9]

The third major problem is the ascription of normative religious status to the nuclear family. It is assumed that God's intended form for the family is a husband (working outside the home), a wife (who is the homemaker), and their immediate offspring living together under one roof, with the husband considered head of the household. Such an understanding, for all its unfairness to other family forms, does not even take history seriously. In fact, it was not until the nineteenth century that the present form of the nuclear family arose, for only then did mobility undercut the extended family, and not until then was mothering seen as a full-time occupation or childhood viewed as a separate era of life. Those who insist that there has been one normative family form simply do not have Christian history on their side.

The antidote for this problem is a time-honored Protestant emphasis: "the Protestant principle." This is the insistence that nothing finite ever be absolutized. It is a reflection of the Decalogue's first commandment, and the realization that when Jesus said that the sabbath was made for persons and not vice versa he was teaching us that every human institution is relative.

In spite of each of these problems, Protestant understandings of marriage and family have struck important positive notes. Marriage is essentially a covenant relationship for which mutuality and companionship are primary values. Thus love is central to its meaning, and procreation of children may be "an added blessing." Valid marriage is not the sole possession of the church, but is open to all. And the building of that small community of intimate support and nurture through which our destiny to communion may be significantly experienced is of inestimable importance for our humanness, though particular family forms themselves are historically relative and changeable.

Protestants generally have upheld the monogamous marriage as the appropriate place for total sexual intimacy. Nevertheless, there is growing recognition that not all premarital sex acts are equally irresponsible. Indeed, if the reality of marriage itself is constituted by the convenanting of the couple, we may need to distinguish between "preceremonial sex" and that sex which takes place outside any meaningful covenant. Adultery is generally condemned by Protestant spokespersons not only because of the significance of intercourse itself and what it symbolizes of God's faithfulness, but also because of probable damage to the marital relationship through deception and the adulteration of love's bonding. Again, however, some Protestants argue that while sexual exclusiveness in marriage is a strong presumptive rule, it is not absolute, for there may be unusual exceptions. What of extramarital sex with the knowledge and consent of the spouse? Though this receives little support, a few Protestant writers argue that *fidelity* is the key issue here, and fidelity is best understood as the bonding of honesty, trust, and primary commitment—which may or may not include genital exclusivity. In all these issues, however, mainline Protestants, while they vary in emphasis, commonly stress the Christian's responsibility to use God's good gift of sexuality in ways that maximize interpersonal fulfillment and faithful intimacy, and that take responsibility for the consequences of sexual acts.

Regarding divorce, Protestants have attempted to take seriously both Jesus' teaching concerning the permanence of marriage and the evidence that life-long unions generally best serve the needs of the marriage partners, their children, and society. Divorce is never to be taken lightly.

Yet Protestants early broke with the medieval Catholic doctrine of the metaphysical indissolubility of marriage, the notion that once the bond between wife and husband had been established it was absolutely incapable of dissolution except by death. Neither the vows spoken, nor the church's blessing, nor sexual intercourse automatically establishes such indissolubility. Jesus' teaching does not imply that what God has joined in principle *cannot* be dissolved. Rather his teaching lays upon the couple and upon society the moral obligation not to frustrate God's purpose of permanent union. Protestants have recognized that marriage breakdown sadly does occur and must be dealt with. If the central meaning of marriage is the covenant of love, then the irreparable breakdown of that covenant— the failure of love—essentially constitutes divorce. If marriage is essentially a moral and not simply a legal union, a personal relation and not a metaphysical construct, then the disintegration of such a relationship must be recognized to prevent further destructiveness to persons.

Successful remarriage to another after divorce, however, is heavily contingent on a creative process wherein persons and their supportive communities honestly face the earlier failures and, through mutual forgiveness, find themselves genuinely divorced from the first union and ready for the second. Without this, the first marriage has not been fully dissolved, but persists as a negative bonding of guilt and resentment, which can only impair the next relationship.[10]

Contraception. If in the last two generations Protes-

89

tants have been champions of family planning and birth control, such was not always the case. The Reformers were as adamant about the obligations of the married to procreate as were their Catholic predecessors. In fact, the religious rivalry that emerged in the sixteenth and seventeenth centuries led Protestant leaders to place a new premium on the reproduction of the faithful. Late nineteenth-century American Protestants supported numerous laws forbidding commerce in contraceptives, and the vision of a Protestant America continued the large-family and anti-contraceptive ideologies.

By 1930, however, medical opinion had shifted from disapproval of contraception to acceptance, and in that year the bishops of the Anglican church at the Lambeth Conference made the first major Protestant statement of endorsement. Not long after, virtually all major Protestant church bodies and theologians publicly supported responsible family-planning through artificial contraception.[11]

The Protestant view that procreation is secondary to love and companionship in marriage and sex undergirded the gradual acceptance of contraception. Openness to modern technology and an emphasis on the nurture of children also helped. Like Roman Catholics, Protestants have argued that each sexual act ought to be "open to the transmission of life," but in distinction from them Protestants have interpreted "life" not in a physical, procreative sense but in the sense of interpersonal life-giving qualities.

Singleness. Historically, the Christian tradition has given its official approval to only two life-styles, monogamous marriage and celibacy. Since Reformation doctrine undercut the notion of meritorious celibacy, Protestants have given comparatively little theoretical attention to the single state. There has been widespread agreement on two counts, however. First, celibacy is to be embraced prior to marriage. Second, when life-long celibacy is chosen because of vocational reasons or personal circumstances and not as a matter of sexual self-rejection or as a quest for special merit, it is to be affirmed. In such cases, the individual is still a sexual being though choosing abstinence from genital relations.

In recent years, Protestant insistence upon complete premarital genital abstinence has become less rigid in many quarters. Part of this is undoubtedly due to changes in cultural attitudes, part of it due to the availability and effectiveness of birth-control and disease-control measures, and part of it due to increased knowledge of psychosexual development. Protestant ethics on this matter now lacks a unified voice, although those who admit the possibility of morally responsible acts of intercourse before marriage typically reserve this to the committed relationship, which is vastly different from an endorsement of unfettered recreational sex.

What of the single adult who does not intend marriage (or remarriage) and who does not choose celibacy? Churches have been notably uncomfortable with adult singles, not only because they raise the sex-outside-marriage issue but also because by their very presence they seem to question marriage as the normative assumption for the Christian life. Furthermore, since so much of the Protestant church's congregational life and education is based on the image of the nuclear family, single adults do not quite seem to fit.

Many Protestants are beginning to recognize, however, that while a single adult's choice to be fully expressive sexually will involve risks, it can be compatible with responsible Christian living. Love's evaluative standards apply here as elsewhere. The relationship should be marked by honesty, genuine commitment, deep respect for the other as a person, caring, and concern for the consequences of intimacy. (I will expand on these issues of singleness in chapter 6.)

Masturbation. Though masturbation is one of the most widely practiced genital expressions of all ages and types of persons, it is still one of the least understood, most guilt-ridden, and least illuminated by Christian reflection. There is no biblical teaching on the subject, though cultural attitudes in biblical times emphasized the importance of procreative sex, on the one hand, and, on the other, attributed to the male semen the presence of life itself. Hence, for the male, masturbation involved the deliberate destruction of human life and the refusal to be procreative.

Churchly condemnation persisted throughout the centuries and was gradually joined by medical opinion, which for several centuries attributed dire physical consequences to the act. Contemporary medical opinion has changed dramatically, however, and attributes no harmful physical effects to masturbation. Since Protestants have not had the Catholic emphasis on the "procreative finality" that must be present or possible in every valid genital act, they are now either silent or divided on the subject.

Some Protestants still find masturbation an intrinsically disordered act, simply because genital expression is divinely intended for interpersonal union. Others find it normal in adolescents and the lesser of evils for single adults or for married persons in the absence of the spouse. Still others find it of little cause for concern unless it becomes a persisting, self-centered choice or a sign of pathological disturbance.

Some Protestants, however, give positive endorsement to masturbation. While it does not have the relational-emotional possibilities of intercourse with the beloved, nevertheless it can be a positive experience of sexual self-exploration and knowledge, of self-affirmation, and of intrapersonal communion. Like other sexual acts, masturbation is susceptible of a whole range of meanings, and its ethical evaluation depends less on the physical act itself than on the constructiveness or destructiveness of its meanings to the person.

Homosexuality. The range of theological and ethical opinion about homosexuality is enormous.[12] Inasmuch as Protestants have considered themselves "a people of the Book," careful biblical interpretation on this issue is imperative. While biblical literalists find in scripture unqualified condemnation of both homosexuality as such and of all homosexual genital acts, other Protestants find differing interpretations more persuasive. Many scholars now agree that there is no clear scriptural message about homosexuality as a psychosexual orientation, for sexual orientation is a distinctly modern concept, foreign to the biblical writers. They also insist that those several passages which clearly refer to homosexual acts must be carefully interpreted in their particular literary, religious, and historical contexts. There appears to be no definitive biblical judgment about same-sex genital expressions of committed love. What we find are various condemnations of homosexual acts in the contexts of idolatry, rape, lust, and promiscuity. Furthermore, in a patriarchal society, male homosexual acts appeared to involve the fruitless loss of the revered semen and also were interpreted as a threat to the status of the male, because one partner in each such act was presumably "womanized."

Nevertheless, even after careful biblical interpretation there remain differences of Protestant conviction. Many argue for a "rejecting-but-nonpunitive" position, believing that homosexuality is unnatural, is contrary to God's design for creation, and cannot be affirmed by Christians. Yet lesbians and gays ought not be treated punitively by the church but rather with a pastoral sensitivity that hopes for their sexual reorientation, if such is possible, and for their chastity if it is not. Other Protestant groups and writers argue for "qualified acceptance." They agree with the former stance that homosexual orientation falls short of God's intent, but acknowledge on the basis of current evidence that such orientation is irreversible in many persons. In those instances, gay men and lesbians should be supported to live out their lives responsibly—in chastity if that is possible, but, if not, in a permanent, monogamous, same-sex relationship.

There is, however, a growing minority Protestant opinion that presses for the full Christian acceptance of homosexuality. This position sees the biblical evidence as inconclusive on the subject itself, but not on the wider issue of sexuality. Though homosexual expression is not biologically procreative and thus cannot realize the secondary intent of sexuality, it is fully capable of realizing sexuality's primary and central purpose: love and responsible intimacy. Thus love's standards and ethical discernments should apply to all persons regardless of sexual orientation. But, further, the church needs to give particular understanding and support to lesbians and gays, who must live in a society still pervaded by homophobia and oppression.

While in the past decade several ordinations of avowed homosexual candidates have been performed in mainline Protestantism (in The Protestant Episcopal Church and in the United Church of Christ), the ordination question remains a heated issue. The majority of Protestant ecclesiastical bodies have either refused to reconsider the issue or have decided it in the negative.

Women and the church. The ordination of women in mainline Protestantism has increased dramatically during the past decade, as has the number of women seminarians. Here the effects of feminism on theological and ecclesiastical patterns has been much more pronounced than in either Roman Catholicism or Judaism. Such effects include the press toward sexually inclusive language, the use of feminine as well as masculine images and metaphors for the divine, an expanded use of the varied senses in worship, the reform of hierarchical male leadership patterns, and support for social justice and equality regardless of sex. Indeed, such feminist-initiated changes are potentially more far-reaching in their implications than any church reform in several centuries. Many feminists believe, and I agree, that we are on the edge of a basic paradigm shift in our ways of viewing the world.

In all these varied ethical considerations, Protestants find themselves with many differences of conviction. That is inevitable in such a pluralistic religious body. But an increasing number, as witnessed by denominational sexual pronouncements within the past decade, are committed to finding sexual understandings that are at once faithful to the biblical witness and faithful to human experience, sexual understandings that place gospel at the center and law at the boundary, understandings that celebrate the mystery of sexuality as a language of love and see in it a fundamental dimension of God's invitation to our humanness.

· 6 ·

Singleness and the Church

To be single and Christian has been both a good-news and a bad-news story. The bad news may be most evident. Single adults frequently feel left out in congregations where so much activity, liturgical language, and educational material are family oriented. Singles are expected to be en route to marriage or, if not, to remain permanently celibate. Singles frequently are thought of as less than whole persons since they are without partners. Single women are still expected to derive their identities from men. A voluntarily single life-style sounds vaguely unchristian, and the stereotype of "the swinging single" seems blatantly so. The pressures felt by single gay men and lesbians are doubly oppressive. All this is bad news for those single adults who want to be involved fully in the life of the church.

Perhaps, as in the fairy tale, the witch's spell can be broken only by playing the music backward. Let us go back into Christian history to reexamine some themes that have encouraged oppressive attitudes toward singleness.

One important theme comes from the Roman Catholic tradition: singleness as a religious vow is a spiritually superior state. At first glance this affirmation would hardly seem oppressive, and yet it has curiously functioned in that way. In Roman Catholic understanding and practice the spiritual superiority of the single person has entailed several preconditions: (1) the individual has never been married; (2) the person is celibate; and (3) the single state is part of a clerical or monastic vocation within the church. Most singles, Catholic or Protestant, simply do not fit all these criteria. In fact, within the Catholic tradition it is commonly assumed that the nonclergy, nonmonastic single ought to marry and produce a family.

The history of this theme is revealing. Whereas the Hebraic tradition emphasized both the obligation and the virtue of marriage and family, the early Christian church broke from this. One reason for this change was the influx of Hellenistic dualism from late classical Greece, wherein a sharp distinction was made between spirit and body. Spirit was viewed as eternal and superior, and body as finite, corruptible, and corrupting.

There is little if any evidence that Jesus was affected by this spiritualistic dualism either in his teachings or attitudes, although the evidence is strong that he remained celibate and single. Those who have attempted to make a case that Jesus was likely married for a period of time prior to his public ministry have done so on the assumptions that Jesus was committed to the Jewish family ideal, that he was not an ascetic, and that we have no historical record of his life between the ages of twelve years and thirty years, during which time a Jewish male normally would be betrothed and married. Nevertheless, the argument from silence is inconclusive. (Certainly Paul would have known if Jesus had been married, and Paul would have mentioned it in his letters.)

In Paul himself there is a mix of both the Hebraic and the Greek influences. Added to this, Paul with other early Christians was awaiting the sudden return of Christ and the inauguration of the "kingdom of God." Hence, he counseled Christians to live on tiptoe, unencumbered by unnecessary earthly distractions. From this perspective comes his belief that it is better to remain single if one can do so without succumbing to the passions of sexual desire.

During the first few centuries of the church, celibacy as an outgrowth of Hellenistic dualism became well entrenched, and with the influence of Neoplatonism, the notion of "the ladder of virtue" was popularized. At the top were the martyrs, followed by celibates on the second rung. When the persecutions ceased and Christianity became the religion of the empire, martyrdom disappeared. Then celibacy emerged in top place on the ladder of virtue.

Thus Jerome, tormented by sexual fantasies, could bless marriage only because marriage produced children who were still virgins. Augustine, who in his young adulthood had sexual relationships and fathered a child, embraced celibacy at the time of his spiritual conversion. Augustine taught that since intercourse was always marked by lust it was inescapably sinful and should be engaged in by married couples only for the purposes of procreation. Even though the race had to be replenished, clearly celibacy was the higher calling, to be permanently vowed along with poverty and obedience for those called to the higher religious life. In the later medieval period, a time of great emphasis on rationality as the essence of human nature, celibacy received another boost by the scholastic theologians. They held a deep suspicion of sexual activity, since at the moment of orgasm all rationality seemed to disappear and the control of the rational will evaporated. If marriage was indeed approved it was because most Christians could not hope to live without the burning of fleshly desire, which then needed to be disciplined within the bonds of marriage.

Thus, while singleness has received strong affirmation within the Roman Catholic tradition, it is the celibate singleness of the one called to the monastic or clerical life. For others, marriage is normative.

One other theme difficult for many contemporary singles also comes from the Catholic tradition: the indissolubility of marriage. In the scholastic theology of the high Middle Ages, the understanding of marriage took a decisive turn. If previously the permanence of marriage was seen as a moral obligation, now it was elevated to a metaphysical doctrine. It was not just that marriages *ought not* be broken by divorce. Now they literally *could not* be dissolved: once married, always married, until the one-flesh, ontological union was broken by the death of the spouse.

Since many singles today are single by reason of divorce, this teaching of the church obviously causes problems. If they are Catholic, they are out of good standing with the church. If their marriage has been annulled by the church, however, they are in good ecclesiastical standing, but it has been purchased at the price of declaring that there never had been any real marriage—a questionable churchly pressure, to say the least. But Protestants are not immune to this understanding. Though never officially endorsed by Protestant bodies, the view has undoubtedly influenced attitudes in a manner that says divorce somehow, unexplainably yet undeniably, diminishes one's worth and stature as a person. Many singles, Protestant as well as Catholic, are today trying to cope with this regrettable understanding thrust upon them by questionable theology.

Now consider the Protestant theological picture. Marriage took on a special flavor during the sixteenth-century Reformation. For one thing, there was a strongly patriarchal cast to the model of Christian marriage. Protestant Reformers returned to the Old Testament for their images of family life, and found there heavily male-dominant patterns. Further, they affirmed the procreative norm as the legitimate meaning of human sexuality. While the natural-law tradition was not nearly as strong within Protestantism as in the Catholic Church, still the Reformers were suspicious of any other purpose for sexual activity beyond that of procreation. A further factor (elevated once again by twentieth-century theologians such as Karl Barth) linked the concept of the image of God with heterosexual union. If God created us "male and female," this must have something to do with the image of God. We are destined for communion in our Creator's intent, and no one of us by ourselves can experience, much less possess, the image of God apart from relationship with another. Furthermore, this relationship must be heterosexual, and it must be solemnized by marriage. Thus went the argument.

As Protestant history moved through the industrial revolution, the nuclear family emerged as the normative family standard. Now the ideal was the husband and the wife with their own biological children living together under one roof in a husband-dominant family pattern. While this family structure stemmed from a complex variety of social factors, it was soon given Protestant blessing.

Thus, in the history of the church, two normative standards emerged: single celibacy and heterosexual marriage. Not even the first of these, however, gives viable support and guidance to today's single Christian adults.

Why is the church still largely uncomfortable with single adults? When singleness is a voluntarily chosen way of life and not a regrettable involuntary state because of a spouse's death, the very existence of the single person seems to question marriage as the normative assumption. If the individual is considered "on the way to marriage" he or she is less of a problem. But if singleness appears to be one's chosen life-style, that person's presence itself articulates a challenge to the assumed norm of marriage.

Furthermore, even when the individual is committed to celibacy, the single state itself seems to raise the sex-outside-of-marriage issue, regarding which the church has always been uncomfortable. Here the unfortunate and unfair stereotype of the "swinging single" comes into play. Moreover, it is often assumed that the power of sex is so strong that it is questionable whether single persons can remain celibate even when they desire to do so.

Another reason for discomfort is that so much of the church's life is organized around a certain image of the family. This image is not of the extended family, nor of a pluralism of family styles, but rather of the nuclear family, which received religious blessing only in the last century. The single adult is not a family person by that definition. Thus, she or he needs to be "adopted" to feel at home at the family-night potluck supper. And when the image of "the family of God" is invoked in Sunday worship, there is a nagging suspicion that those who conform more fully to the experience of the approved earthly family are more fully members of God's own family.

Still another reason for the church's problem with singleness is its inability to cope theologically and ethically with the issue of self-love. At the time of the Reformation, Protestant theology, in an attempt to accent the splendor of God's undeserved grace, began to express an unfortunate dichotomy in its understanding of love. The contrast was drawn between agape and eros. Agape, it was believed, was divine in its origin, utterly selfless and self-giving. Eros, however, was believed to be an acquisitive and selfish form of love, concerned only for the needs and satisfactions of the individual. Self-love, by definition, was a form of eros—selfish and unchristian. While the theologians did not draw the argument out in ways oppressive to single persons, the implication has remained. If one must be loved in order to be whole, and if that love ideally comes from both divine and human sources, and if self-love is illegitimate for Christians, single persons are assumed to be deficient in their experience of love and wholeness—simply because they are without a spouse.

Thus, regardless of gender or sexual orientation, the

single adult poses particular problems for the rest of the church. Because of a continuing double standard in sexual ethics, younger heterosexual males automatically seem to raise the sex-outside-of-marriage issue in the eyes of others, for they are assumed to be sexually active. Though this assumption is less strongly directed toward the single heterosexual woman, in a different way she automatically violates a norm, for she is not properly receiving her authentication and identity from a male, an important norm of the patriarchal mind set. Lesbians and gay males, whether celibate or not, automatically offend against the sex-is-for-procreation tradition and against the assumption that the nuclear family is the proper form of relational existence.

For a variety of reasons, then, the nonsingle part of the church has had a difficult time fully embracing singles. If some of the reasons for this never surface to the level of consciousness, they nevertheless function with considerable power.

Now, however, it is time to move to the good news. We are undergoing an important paradigmatic shift in our understanding of sexuality. The shift is not neat. It is not happening all at once, nor is the new pattern without its roots in the past. But the contrasts are emerging, and they are real. If the old paradigm was committed to a body-spirit dualism, the new vision believes in the wholeness of the self (knowing that wholeness and holiness, health and healing, are all linked linguistically and in fact with salvation). If the old pattern was committed to a sexist and patriarchal dualism, the new one is committed to equality and androgyny. If the old paradigm embraced the procreative norm as the legitimating reason for sexual relationships, the new view believes that love is the norm of sexual existence. If the old pattern saw celibacy and heterosexual marriage as the only legitimate forms of Christian life, the new mode affirms a plurality of valid Christian styles. If the old way of believing saw sexuality as either incidental or actually detrimental to the human-divine relationship, the new paradigm sees sexuality as a positive dimension of our humanness and as intrinsic to the human-divine relationship.

What, then, are the theological resources for single wholeness? A number of affirmations may be particularly important. Let me sketch just a few of them.

The journeying God. One of the basic biblical insights (frequently lost, however, in academic theology and popular piety) is that God is always on the move. God is always calling the people to journey into a new land. We live in tents and not in an abiding earthly city. The journeying God creates in us a kind of faith that means a permanent revolution of all our cherished concepts.

One implication of this ongoing revolution is the conviction that all our institutional structures are relative and must not be absolutized. If God is constantly calling us to move toward a new age, then to absolutize any given structure is a mark of unfaith. The nuclear family, which many Christians believe to be the permanent, unalterable, divinely inspired form for the family, in actuality did not develop until the late nineteenth century. While this family form has served many persons well and may continue to do so, it is not the once-and-for-all model of family existence.

Single persons need families. And single persons can be part of families in significant ways. But often these families will not be of the traditional nuclear model. The family may not have blood ties or legal ties. It may be comprised of several close friends bonded together in implicit covenant and experience; it may be a lover or a close friend with whom there is no specifically sexual relationship; or it may be a same-sex support group. Jesus himself intimated that family ties are both important *and* relative when he asked, "Who are my mother and my brothers? [Mark 3:33]."

The androgynous God. A persisting obstacle to the affirmation of single persons is the mistaken notion that gender complementarity is necessary if one is to experience the image of God. One problem with this notion is that it assumes and perpetuates unfortunate sex-role stereotypes. It assumes that one is biologically fated to a restricted range of emotional and intellectual characteristics, and as such needs the close complementarity of the opposite sex to make one human whole.

Even more basic is the distortion of the perception of God. While it is clear that the statistically dominant images for God in the Bible and Christian tradition are masculine, Christians are discovering that this does an idolatrous injustice to God. God embraces both genders as well as transcends them. As we become accustomed to the richness of female and feminine metaphors for God as well as male and masculine ones, we will become more fully human in our own androgynous capacities. No one of us was intended to be only half human. No one of us was intended to be either autonomous or dependent, but with the capacities for both: not simply either rational or intuitive, but with the ability to embrace both; not simply either assertive or receptive, but with the capacity for both ways of relating.

The importance for single persons is perhaps obvious. Without denigrating the richness many find in marriage, we can affirm that no individual absolutely needs another of the opposite gender in order to be whole. To assume this would do injustice both to God and to human nature.

A model of Jesus who was both single and whole. It is

104

striking that those who argue most vigorously that gender complementarity is necessary for human wholeness apparently have not noticed that in so doing they are excluding Jesus. To assume that such relationship is necessary for everyone else except Jesus is to make of him a Docetic exception to genuine humanity and thus to deny the radical meaning of incarnation.

On the contrary, the New Testament picture of Jesus is a compelling portrait of wholeness in a single person. If the argument that Jesus was at one time married and then widowed is not terribly persuasive, that argument does serve a critical purpose. By seriously examining the evidence we are taking the argument itself seriously, and in so doing we are affirming that Jesus' humanity was fully sexual. The evidence is most persuasive that Jesus was celibate. Refraining from genital relationships, nevertheless he was deeply in touch with his own embodiedness, his feelings, his sensuous capacities, his eros. All this is evident in his relationships with others, both women and men. It is evident in the passion that pervaded his life. Our sexuality is much more than genitality. For many persons sexuality will include genital relationships. For some it will not, and yet they may be fully and richly sexual beings. Our sexuality is essentially our embodied eros toward intimacy and communion. As such it is a fundamental dimension of our selfhood, and Jesus appears to be a striking model of one who was both single and whole.

An understanding of relationship as the essence of selfhood. Martin Buber, the great Jewish philosopher and theologian, used the striking phrase, "In the beginning is the relation." He did not say "in the beginning is God," nor "in the beginning is being itself." Rather, relationship is the stuff that constitutes the meaning of everything, even in the beginning. Physically, emotionally, intellectually, spiritually, and culturally we are literally fated to be social selves. We find our own authenticity, our own power, our own capacity for creativity and love when we are most fully in touch with others.

To experience relationship as the essence of selfhood does not mean that we must marry (though for some it will mean that). It does not mean that all must be heterosexual (though the majority will probably be that). It does not mean that one must have genital relationships (though the majority perhaps will have them). Relationship as the essence of selfhood simply and profoundly means that we are most fully ourselves when we are most deeply related to others, both to God and to the creaturely neighbor.

A significant development took place in the history of Christian sexuality in seventeenth-century Protestantism. Prior to that time it had been assumed by the teachers of the church that procreation was either the primary or the only legitimate purpose of genital sexuality. During the seventeenth century the (much-maligned) Puritans together with some Quakers and Anglicans began to articulate their conviction that the purpose of sexuality was not fundamentally procreation but that of relationship, companionship, and love. If in marriage children were born, that was to be seen as an added blessing. But the purpose of marriage was not primarily to beget children. It was to form a bonding of companionship and love.

This is an important clue for singles as well as for those who choose marriage. We are all sexual beings. Our sexuality is God's magnificent and ingenious gift to implant within us the desire for intimacy and relationship, whether this is genitally expressed or not. Our sexuality is both the physiological and the psychological grounding of our capacity to love. The abiding clue of embodied selves is that our destiny is for fulfilling relationships.

The positive resource of self-love. As I have mentioned,

Christianity has had a difficult time understanding the positive necessity and gift of self-love, a love that is fundamentally different from narcissism or selfishness. The church and its theologians have seldom recognized the demons of self-hate that are loose in our lives and in our world. All too frequently, Christian thought has encouraged a certain kind of masochism as the mark of true discipleship.

With the help of both modern psychology and more careful theological reflection, we are beginning to realize that love is indivisible and nonquantifiable. It simply is not true that the more love one has for one's self, the less one will have for others. These are not viable alternatives. Jesus did not enjoin us to love our neighbors *instead* of ourselves, but *as* ourselves. Without experiencing a profound and genuine self-acceptance and a grateful affirmation of our own worth, it is very difficult indeed genuinely to affirm others. If we cannot say yes to ourselves, it is very difficult for us to say yes to another.

While these affirmations are of basic importance to everyone, they may have a special significance for singles. Single adults may more frequently be thrown back on their own resources. The single person may need to cope more frequently with times of aloneness and, perhaps, loneliness. While this is not the case for all, many singles know these experiences and by the same token know the great importance of positive self-regard and self-affirmation.

In regard to genital expression, only by a strong affirmation of the importance of positive self-love can a healthy affirmation be made of physical self-love. The person who chooses to be genitally expressive and who also has a positive attitude about his or her own body has the possibility of rewarding experiences of self-touch, self-pleasuring, and masturbation. While such physical self-love is not of course limited to single persons, it may be of particular significance to those singles who choose to be celibate in their relations with others. Masturbation is not inherently immature, narcissistic, or sick. Unfortunately, the church has not yet done its homework well on either the emotional or the physical dimensions of positive self-love. But it is beginning to do so, and this is another resource for the single person.

The grace of God. In the Christian gospel, grace is the first word and the last word. God's radical acceptance of us is traditionally known as justification by grace. God's power within us, enabling new growth and wholeness, is traditionally called sanctification by grace. Justification means that we are profoundly accepted in whatever condition, whatever relationship, whatever sexual orientation, whatever record of past purity or irresponsibility we have. God's capacity to elicit new growth and wholeness within us, nurturing more self-acceptance, sensuousness, and androgyny, and the capacity for integrating all our lives around the meanings of love—these are resources of fundamental importance for everyone.

Because human beings are destined for community as well as created by and in community, the Christian faith has always had a high doctrine of the church. It is part of the church's shame in our time that so many single persons have found less than a full welcome and inclusion in its common life. But the church has the potential to embrace more fully the resources described above so that it can be a communal home and a body of journeying companions for everyone, single and married, homosexual and heterosexual, young and old, never married and re-singled.

I end on a personal note. As one who has been married for thirty years, I have few special credentials to write an essay on singleness. Nevertheless, particularly in recent years I have been challenged by the strength, the vulnerability, the anger, and the searching of numerous single Christians. My consciousness has been raised in ways that I would not have imagined a few years ago concerning the oppression that the church has, often quite unconsciously, visited upon them. I want to be part of the church's repentance. I deeply want the church to be an inclusive and enriching community for all.

Beyond this, single Christians have an important witness to those who are married and paired. Singles can remind others of us that no relationship, however ecclesiastically and legally sanctioned, no matter how many years of duration, will be life-giving when there is not the strength of individuality in each of its partners. When love's bonds become possessive, when love's bonds become stifling and enslaving, what once promised life now delivers death. Singles can remind the paired and married that there is no one form of life to which everyone is called. Rather, there are many different patterns and lifestyles that need to be woven into the rich tapestry of shared Christian existence.

· 7 ·

Religious and Moral Issues in Working with Homosexual Counselees

*A*t the outset, let me offer a linguistic comment. I consider the word *homosexuality* an abstraction. There is no such thing as homosexuality per se. When I use the term I am speaking about people who happen to be more or less erotically oriented to their own sex; people who are more or less comfortable with this orientation; and people who experience more or fewer difficulties, personal and social, because of their orientation. I am always speaking of concrete persons, in spite of the limitations of language.[1]

Can a Counselor Be Neutral?

Can a counselor or therapist, whatever her or his own sexual orientation, be neutral when working with homosexual clients? Quite apart from the question of sexual orientation, when the general issue of religious and moral neutrality in counseling is considered, a distinction is sometimes made between pastoral counseling and secular psychotherapy. The former is assumed to be interlaced with normative values and religious beliefs, since clergy are expected in all their ministerial functions to represent and interpret the meanings of the religious group. In contrast, many people assume that the secular psychotherapist (whether or not committed to a religious tradition) will take an educative, counseling approach. The therapist will not attempt to impose solutions but, maintaining a neutral standpoint, will attempt to educe both emotional and moral solutions from the client.

This neat division, however, is highly misleading. In recent decades many clergy have moved toward substantially psychotherapeutic models of counseling, attempting to keep their own religious and moral convictions very much in the background. At the same time, it is increasingly recognized that the professional psychotherapist is not dealing with a religiously or morally neutral process. Psychotherapy, like religion, tries to help people change their lives. In assisting clients to alleviate their emotional distress, the therapist necessarily operates with certain images of "sin" (the causative factors and dynamics of the distress), certain images of "salvation" (the dynamics of change, the hoped-for cure or pattern of growth), and some general interpretation of human fulfillment and life's meaning.[2]

If these observations are true of counseling in general, it is even clearer that religious and moral neutrality are impossible when one is working with homosexual clients. Although counselors will vary in the extent to which they allow their own convictions to enter the process, I believe it neither possible nor desirable for them to escape altogether a whole series of moral and religious questions, the answers to which will critically affect the pattern and course of the counseling or therapy. Is homosexuality as such good, bad, or neutral? Are certain difficulties frequently encountered by gay men and lesbians intrinsic to their sexual orientation, or are they rooted in the dynamics of social oppression? What are the ethics of genital expression, and are these criteria the same for both homosexual and heterosexual persons? What are the purposes of human sexuality? How does one assess the varied Western religious traditions on the issue of homosexuality? Are clients likely to be helped or hindered by their particular religious belief systems and involvements? As these questions, and others, will be answered in one way or another by counselors, it is important that they be clear about their own commitments and knowledgeably sensitive to particular issues commonly faced by gay men and lesbians.

The following discussion will reflect a number of my own convictions, which I have attempted to elaborate elsewhere: that homosexuality is a valid orientation for Christians; that homosexual genital expression should be guided by the same general ethical criteria that are appropriate for heterosexual expression, though with sensitivity to the special situation of an oppressed minority; that the church, while too frequently a participant in oppression, does have important healing resources for gay men and lesbians; and that the church deeply needs the gay and lesbian presence and witness.[3]

Understanding the Religious Tradition

No gay or lesbian in our society can escape responding in some manner to the ways the Judeo-Christian tradition has dealt with homosexuality. Likewise, it is predictable that numerous gay and lesbian counselors will be working on issues of self-worth and self-esteem stemming from condemnation by organized religion. Whether the biblical and theological arguments are of personal concern to the counselor is beside the point. They *do* matter to many gay and lesbian clients. Accordingly, it can be enormously helpful if the counselor is able to respond knowledgeably to the question "But doesn't the Bible say homosexuality is a sin?" with "No, not as I understand it."

Fortunately, a number of books and articles now available afford reliable, detailed treatment of the biblical and theological issues. My purpose here is limited to a summary overview.

Any specific biblical passage relating to homosexuality must, I believe, be interpreted with several things in mind. First, homosexuality *as a psychosexual orientation* is not dealt with in the Bible. The concept of sexual orientation is distinctly modern. The Bible's references are, without exception, statements about certain types of same-sex *acts*. In all probability, the biblical writers assumed that all persons were "naturally" heterosexual; hence, those who engaged in homosexual activity were doing so in willful and conscious violation of their own (heterosexual) natures.

Second, the strong link between sex and procreation, particularly in the Old Testament, must be understood in a particular historical context. A small Hebrew tribe in a hostile environment indeed needed children for its survival.

Third, both Old and New Testaments (though I believe they also contain a doctrine of radical human equality) were admittedly written in the context of male-dominated societies. The issue of *male* homosexual activity receives virtually all the attention, for lesbian activity hardly constitutes the same threat to the patriarchal mind set.

Fourth, coupled with the procreative emphasis and patriarchal assumptions, there was a biological misunderstanding. The prescientific (male) mind, knowing nothing of eggs and ovulation and assuming a special life-transmitting power for the semen alone, frequently concluded that deliberate nonprocreative expulsion of semen was a serious, life-destroying act.

Fifth, biblical references to homosexual acts almost always reflect a genuine anxiety about idolatrous religious practices. In the ancient Mideast, idolatry frequently found sexual expression. In such practices (both heterosexual and homosexual), sex was depersonalized and seen as a mysterious power that one must dedicate to the deity out of fear.

Given these contextual factors, what might we make of the specific biblical passages? The answer, in short, is: not very much. In the vast spectrum of biblical material there are surprisingly few references to homosexual acts, and almost all of these speak to religious and social conditions significantly different from our own. Consider, briefly, the most frequently cited texts (and those with which most gay and lesbian clients have had personally to deal).

The destruction of Sodom and Gomorrah (Genesis 19), though often believed to show God's condemnation of homosexual activity, cannot fairly be interpreted in this manner. In recent decades, many noted biblical scholars have concluded that "the sin of Sodom" was in fact the general violation of Hebraic standards of social justice, including the violation of the norm of hospitality to the stranger. Even if one grants a primarily sexual focus to the story, the only reasonable conclusion is that here are condemnations of sexual intercourse with divine messengers and of violent gang rape, but not condemnations of other forms of homosexual genital activity or of homosexuality as an orientation.

In two other Old Testament passages, however, there are unmistakable denunciations of homosexual acts, both explicitly male in reference. Leviticus 18:23 and 20:13, part of the Holiness Code, reflect an overriding concern for the separateness and purity of God's chosen people, in contrast to the surrounding tribes with their idolatrous practices, including the use of female and male temple prostitutes. Selective literalists today frequently single out these texts, forget (or are unaware of) their historical context, and ignore the numerous other proscriptions in the same code, such as those against eating rare meat, having marital intercourse during menstruation, and wearing clothing of mixed fabrics.

The New Testament contains no recorded words of Jesus on the subject. Its principal references are those of Paul in Romans 1:24–27 and 1 Corinthians 6:9–10, and of the "Pauline" writer of 1 Timothy 1:8–11. The latter two texts deal with types of activity which, it was believed, warranted excluding persons from the reign of God. Both passages, however, need careful linguistic interpretation and, when given it, appear not to be directed toward all homosexual persons but rather to specific kinds of homosexual acts, namely exploitation, homosexual prostitution, and the sexual use of boys by adult males.

Paul's words in Romans 1 are usually taken as the strongest New Testament rejection of homosexuality. (Here is the one and only biblical reference to female as well as male same-sex activity.) Paul, however, speaks specifically of same-sex acts that express idolatry and acts undertaken in lust (not tenderness or mutual respect) by heterosexuals who willfully act contrary to their own sexual natures. I am not inferring that the apostle necessarily would have approved of other kinds of same-sex acts. I am simply arguing that it is inaccurate and unfair to interpret his words as directed to nonexploitive and loving acts by same-sex couples for whom mutual homosexual attraction is part of the given of *their* natures.

Counselees and their counselors, therefore, need to be aware that careful examination of the biblical material renders no definitive scriptural word on homosexuality as a sexual orientation or upon homosexual genital expression in a relationship of respect and love. Specifically, the Bible contains several references to certain kinds of same-sex acts in religious and cultural contexts quite different from most of those faced by gay men and lesbians today.

Often forgotten, too, is the manner in which scripture celebrates instances of genuine love between two men or two women: David and Jonathan, Ruth and Naomi, Jesus and the Beloved Disciple.

Beyond all this, a Christian approach counsels its adherents to assess every moral judgment (whether made by ancient Hebrews or later by Christians) in terms of the spirit of love and to recognize that the central question is not what constitutes a breach of divine moral law as understood in certain historical periods, but rather what constitutes responsive faithfulness to God, the Cosmic Lover revealed in Jesus Christ. The Bible conveys the message that human sexuality is one of the Creator's great and good gifts, to be integrated fully into one's personhood and expressed in ways that honor both God and the human partner.

Dealing with Current Theological Opinion and Church Practice

The scriptural questions by themselves do not exhaust the theological issues with which many gay men and lesbians must deal. The church has a long and unfortunate history of homosexual oppression that continues into the present. As John Boswell's impressive scholarship has demonstrated, Christianity's opposition to homosexuality was not original but derived from non-Christian sources.[4] Nor has the opposition always been consistent. There were centuries of tolerance. Nevertheless, most of today's gay men and lesbians have met with substantially more rejection than affirmation by the church.

Two theological issues in particular frequently surface in counseling. One is the claim that the homosexual orientation itself is contrary to nature, or to natural law, or to God's intention in creation. To the extent that this is internalized, counselees will probably regard themselves as freakish and unnatural in this very fundamental way. Frequently, of course, the "unnatural" label is coupled with psychological notions of illness, perversion, and arrested development, or even with religious notions of idolatry.

The religiously sensitive counselor can assist in more than one way. First, there is the cognitive process of sorting out the natural law argument. Several points deserve attention. One is the grounding of this argument in a static metaphysical world view that appeared appropriate to the Middle Ages but is quite inappropriate today. Now we recognize that there is no fixed human nature that can be read from the structure of human biology. Because human beings are constantly in the process of becoming, the definition of what is naturally human is forever being modified and changed. Even within the Roman Catholic Church, which has been most heavily committed to natural law, many theologians affirm this. Thus, Fr. Gregory Baum argues that what is normative is the human nature toward which we are divinely summoned: the life of mutuality, in terms of which homosexual love is not to be excluded or seen as contradictory.[5]

Related to the above are the biological assertions that procreation is the primary purpose of sex and that, since homosexual intercourse is by definition nonprocreative, it is unnatural and contrary to creation. Mainstream Protestant thought began to move away from the primacy-of-procreation position three centuries ago; more recently much Roman Catholic thought has done likewise. Indeed, the church has always recognized the validity of the marriage in which sterility made procreation impossible, and since 1931 the Catholic Church has officially endorsed lovemaking without baby-making through approval of the rhythm method of birth control. If the primary purpose of sexual expression is communion or love, then it is difficult to exclude any type of nonprocreative lovemaking, hetero-

117

sexual or homosexual. The central question is inescapable: What is the fundamental meaning of our sexuality?

Finally, it should be remembered by both counselor and counselee that most natural-law arguments against homosexuality, whether they articulate them or not, rest on an assumption of gender complementarity. It is assumed that men and women are naturally constituted with essentially different personality configurations (e.g., men are cognitive, women are intuitive, etc.), so that one sex is incomplete until it finds its complement in the other. But this notion is based on disproven sex-role stereotypes, covertly supports an unjust dominance-submission relation between the sexes, and allows neither sex to develop its androgynous possibilities. What the argument misses, in short, is the uniqueness of human personality. We are, indeed, destined for communion with others. We do, indeed, find our loneliness assuaged and our deficiencies met with another's strengths. But this can be the case for the homosexual as well as the heterosexual couple. It is not biologically destined.

Closely related to and overlapping the above natural-law arguments is a position officially subscribed to by several major church bodies today. It holds that while homosexuality as an *orientation* is contrary to God's created intention, the homosexual *person* ought not to be adversely judged or rejected by the church. Often this position carries the acknowledgment that sexual orientation is seldom if ever the result of voluntary choice and that constitutional homosexuality appears largely unsusceptible to psychotherapeutic reorientation. While this is a more tolerant and compassionate view than outright condemnation, it places gay men and lesbians in two impossible binds.

One, of course, is the internal recognition that one's own sexual orientation is as natural and as fundamental to one's identity as is skin color. It is both naive and cruel to tell a lesbian or gay man, "Your sexual orientation is still unnatural and a perversion, but this is no judgment upon you as a person." The individual knows otherwise.

The other bind concerns churchly pressure toward celibacy. When the church presumes to be nonjudgmental toward homosexual orientation but then prohibits any genital expression, it is difficult to understand how the sense of guilt, even in the celibate, will be significantly alleviated. In most lesbians and gay men it is likely and understandable that anger will increase, for they will see this as churchly hypocrisy.

In the face of these conflicts, counselor and counselee need to realize two important things. One is that there are both intellectual and psychological contradictions in any position based either on an outmoded version of natural law or on a sharp distinction between sexual orientation and genital expression.

The second recognition is equally important: there is a significant and increasing pluralism within organized Christianity on these issues. Theologians and churches, Protestant and Catholic, simply do not have a unified mind, and the counselee needs to know this. In spite of the official Vatican position, there are distinguished Catholic theologians who publicly proclaim homosexuality as valid for Christians, and there are creative and affirming Catholic ministries to gay and lesbian communities. Within Protestantism, the spectrum is even greater. Here, too, one can find an increasing number of church leaders giving full affirmation to lesbians and gay men—not only among liberals but now also among those who identify themselves as evangelical.

There have been ordinations of publicly affirmed gay and lesbian persons in at least two major Protestant denominations and vigorous debate about the issue in others. In recent years, several national church groups have undertaken major studies of human sexuality, occasioning considerable reassessment of traditional attitudes about homosexuality. Furthermore, since 1968 there have arisen gay and lesbian organizations within virtually every major American denomination. A new movement, the Metropolitan Community Churches, with ministries and congregations organized primarily by and for gay men and lesbians, has become a rapidly expanding urban religious phenomenon in this country and abroad, and is en route to becoming a denomination recognized by others.

Particularly within the last dozen years there has been a vigorous ferment about homosexual issues in American church life. In every case, except the most conservative and fundamentalist groups, this ferment has produced new openness toward and affirmation of lesbians and gay men. If, as is sadly true, the legacy of rejection is still alive, it is also true that changes are occurring in the churches as never before in recent centuries. It would be a mistake for any counselor or counselee to assume that the church is a monolithic and condemning entity.

Questions Surrounding Gay/Lesbian Spirituality and Life-Style

It is probable that proportionately fewer lesbians than gay men are still attempting to find a spiritual home in the organized church. After all, in spite of some encouraging progress on feminist issues, the churches are still unquestionably male-dominated. Hence, lesbians have two strikes against them—gender as well as sexual orientation—and, feeling their powerlessness in the church, a number have voted with their feet. For those lesbians and gays who still seek a religious life within organized Christian communions, what are the important resources for their wholeness and mental health?

One resource is the experience of community. While

never perfectly present, it is there in some measure for gays and lesbians in some congregations. The internalization of such labels as "sinner," "sick," and "unnatural" inevitably leads to shame and guilt, and thence to social withdrawal. The need for a community of acceptance and affirmation more personally inclusive than can be found in bars and baths is real. That this enormously important resource does exist for gay men and lesbians, at least in some churches, ought not to be overlooked. When the religious community can assist the coming-out process, help to mitigate its pain, and help the individual to celebrate new openness, the rewards are particularly great inasmuch as the energy drain and encouragement toward self-rejection in a closeted person forced to live a double life take a heavy toll.

Feelings of guilt over homosexuality can be exacerbated to a point of moral scrupulosity by the internalization of negative attitudes toward sexuality itself. A positive, indeed celebrative, religious attitude toward human sexuality, then, is another resource possible within the church. Even though much of the church throughout much of its history has been remiss on this score, the foundations for sexual affirmation are central to Christianity's theological tenets. Christianity is a religion of incarnation, and an incarnationalist faith affirms the body as good. We can be both fully spiritual and fully sexual; indeed, that is our destiny.

If the majority of Christians have internalized some sex-negative attitudes from their religion, lesbians and gay men have been susceptible to an even heavier dose than have heterosexuals. Forced by a hostile majority to defend their sexual orientation, gay people are more likely to internalize feelings of shame simply because of *being sexual*. It is therefore difficult to overestimate the importance of the counselor's awareness of the need for positive religious approaches to sexuality. To be sure, our salvation (or health or wholeness—the words all have the same root) is always incomplete. Because none of us is whole, the unhealed parts of our sexuality will continue to hurt others and ourselves. But the homosexual counselee needs to know (no less than and no more than does the heterosexual counselee) that the fundamental word of the Christian message is grace: grace as God's radical acceptance and grace as God's empowerment for new life and growth. The gracious Word has been made flesh, and our flesh is confirmed.

A church which believes that God's grace yearns for its fullest possible human embodiment will strive to help all persons to affirm and celebrate their sexuality. It is, after all, God's gift which makes communion and intimacy possible. And, if these things are true, then those churches and Christians who would pressure homosexual persons to deny or hide or suppress or refrain from expressing their homosexuality are depriving them of something very fundamental to their wholeness. Churches, rather, should help lesbians and gay men to affirm and to celebrate their homosexuality. It is just as natural to them as is heterosexuality to other persons. And it is just as significant to their wholeness as is heterosexuality to those oriented in that direction. For the churches to believe and to act in this way would truly be a prophetic witness to a homophobic society.

What does all this mean for a moral life-style for the religiously sensitive gay or lesbian? Celibacy is an option to be honored when voluntarily chosen for positive rather than negative reasons. If celibacy is embraced not out of the belief that homosexual genital expression is intrinsically wrong, nor out of generalized fear of sex and intimacy, nor because celibacy is believed to be religiously more meritorious, but rather is embraced because celibacy best expresses the person's own sense of integrity or vocational commitments, it should be genuinely supported.

The celibate is still "a sexual celibate" whose positively affirmed sexuality, while not genitally expressed with another, is the grounding of emotional richness and interpersonal intimacy.[6]

But celibacy ought not to be considered the only valid homosexual life-style for Christians. In addition to the biologism that sex and erotic love are moral only when they are potentially procreative, there is a second major Christian tradition. It might be called the transcendent approach to sexuality, for it strives to transcend biological determinations of eroticism and love.[7] It will surprise many to learn that this latter approach has more New Testament grounding than the former and was, in fact, dominant in theology for several centuries in the early Christian era (a time when, significantly, ecclesiastical opposition to homosexuality was rare). If current secular society is now ahead of the church in its tolerance of "nonbiological" love (at least between heterosexuals), the church needs to reclaim its earlier tradition and not capitulate to the fears of ultraconservative Christians who would move us back into an even more stringent biological determinism.

Human sexuality, for all its similarity to animal sexuality, is not under the tyranny of biology. Our sexuality is highly symbolic in its meanings and capable of expressing the depths of human self-understanding and desires for relatedness. Our sexuality is capable of expressing and sharing a total personal relationship that contributes immeasurably toward our intended destiny as human beings, that of lovers after the image of the Cosmic Lover.

Hence, the core issue for sexual ethics is not the assessment of certain types of physical acts as right or wrong. Abnormality or deviance ought not to be defined statistically, but rather in reference to the Christian norm—authentic humanity as revealed in Jesus as Christ. Gay men and lesbians desire and need deep, lasting rela-

123

tionships no less than do heterosexual people, and appropriate genital expression should be denied to neither.

Thus, the appropriate ethical question is this: What sexual behavior will serve and enhance, rather than inhibit and damage, the fuller realization of our divinely intended humanity? The answer, I believe, is sexual behavior in accordance with love. This means commitment, trust, tenderness, respect for the other, and the desire for responsible communion. It means resisting cruelty, utterly impersonal sex, obsession with sexual gratification, and actions that display unwillingness to take responsibility for their personal and social consequences. This kind of ethic is equally appropriate to both heterosexual and homosexual Christians.

But this statement deserves a word of qualification. The social and religious oppression experienced by most gay men and lesbians has driven some, especially men, to rely heavily on the satisfactions of impersonal sex associated with cruising, the gay baths, and "tea rooms." While there is no homosexual monopoly on impersonal sex, it is understandably a greater temptation when the majority society does everything possible to discourage lasting homosexual unions and when most of the church refuses to bless and support the covenants of gay or lesbian couples. Given the realities of social oppression, it is insensitive and unfair to judge simply by a heterosexual ideal of monogamy, and many gays and lesbians, quite understandably, resist the imposition of a heterosexual norm which is so frequently broken. What can be said to everyone regardless of orientation is this: genital expression will find its greatest fulfillment in a relationship of ongoing commitment and communion. That other sexual experiences can have elements of genuine good in them, even when they do not realize the fullest meanings of personal intimacy, remains an open possibility.

For the gay or lesbian couple who intend a covenant

of indefinite duration, will fidelity always mean genital exclusivity? Some couples (as is true of some heterosexuals) have explored the possibility of sexual intimacy with secondary partners. For these couples, infidelity does not have a simple biological meaning. Rather, it means the rupture of the bonds of faithfulness, trust, honesty, and commitment. On the positive side, fidelity is understood as enduring commitment to the partner's well-being and growth, a commitment to the primacy of this covenant over any other relationship. While there are undoubted risks in expanding the boundaries of physical intimacy, and while the weight of Christian tradition is on the side of sexual exclusivity, there are also risks to a couple's relationship when it becomes marked by possessiveness or emotional dependence.

These, then, are guidelines and ideals that can assist the religiously sensitive individual to make decisions about appropriate genital expression. They are guidelines, however, and not legalisms. They respect the necessity of personal choice, and they include a Christian understanding of forgiveness and the possibility of new beginnings when an individual's sexual expression becomes more destructive than creative.

Homophobia and the Church's Need for Gay and Lesbian Christians

Thus far my emphasis has been on the resources that gay men and lesbians might find within the Christian faith. What remains to be emphasized is the need of other Christians to have homosexual brothers and sisters within the religious community. Churches and society both desperately need release from homophobia, the irrational fear of same-sex orientation and expression.

Some resistance to homosexuality is, to be sure, based

on calm and reasoned religious belief; undoubtedly much is also based on unreasoned, ill understood emotional reactions. It would otherwise be difficult to understand the persistence of selective biblical literalism and long-disproven homosexual stereotypes among so many church members.

While homophobia can be accounted for by a variety of psychodynamics, including the projection of fears about homosexual feelings in the self, its deep roots in the twin forms of alienating sexual dualism need also to be recognized. Spiritualistic dualism (spirit over body) is likely to be present. Virtually everyone in our society suffers from the internally divisive effects of spiritualism and longs for (in unconscious as well as conscious ways) the essential reunion of the body-self. Since stereotypes insist that gay men and lesbians are more sexually defined and simply more sexual than heterosexual men and women, they become the targets of subconscious envy. Homosexuality becomes the symbol of exciting and sensual sexuality which (it is assumed) too many people would choose if they were given permission. Hence the stereotype bears an unintended harvest that gives a powerful dynamic to homophobia.

As I have noted in earlier chapters, the dynamic of sexist dualism may be even stronger than spiritualistic dualism. Consider the predominance of biblical concern with *male* homosexuality. Male homosexuality appears to threaten "normal" masculine gender identity. It calls into question the dominance-submission patterns of any patriarchal society as well as the myths of supermasculinism by which that society lives. Unconsciously, the heterosexual male seems to fear that his acceptance of male homosexuality in others would open him to the risk of "womanization." The same male resents the man-to-man emotional intimacy and affirmation symbolized by gays but denied to heterosexual men who have been conditioned to relate competitively and superficially to other men.

Thus not only gay men and lesbians but surely also heterosexual people in the church and in society have enormous benefits to gain by freeing themselves from the destructive dynamics of homophobia. Insofar as this occurs, everyone will find release from dehumanizing sex-role stereotypes. We will discover liberation from fears about the continuum of sexual feelings within the self. We will experience more genuine self-acceptance and self-affirmation, and with greater relational equality. We will have enriched possibilities for intimate friendships with fewer debilitating sexual fears between the sexes, as well as in same-sex friendship patterns. We can expect a diminution of male-biased social violence in its myriad forms. We will enjoy more permission for each of us to develop her or his own human uniqueness. And the churches will learn more of the heart of the Christian message, including the freedom, inclusiveness, and justice that come from taking incarnate grace seriously.

Gay men and lesbians need to know how much everyone in society will benefit from the gains in their own struggle for liberation. While it is grossly unfair to place the burden of liberating the oppressors upon the oppressed, it may be that the latter can find augmented self-assurance in knowing how deeply they are needed by the former.

· 8 ·

The Family: Some Theses
for Discussion

*I*t was Will Rogers, I believe, who gave this sobering bit of advice: "Folks who gaze into crystal balls ought to have them shoved down their throats." Mindful of the significant debates among social scientists about the future of the family, and mindful of my own limitations for entering that debate, I will not attempt an analysis of the future of this basic social institution. Rather, I will simply propose some theses for discussion. These propositions, of course, rest upon certain sociological assumptions, but even more they reflect certain theological and ethical convictions. I propose seven of them (a good biblical number):

1. The family is neither dead nor dying.
2. The greater pluralism of family forms, now emerging, can be a good thing.
3. Marriage is more a process than a state of being.
4. The fear of sexuality is one of the family's greatest enemies.
5. Love is the central meaning of marriage and family.
6. The family is called to be an agency for the transformation of the world.
7. The grace of God is fundamental to all the above.

1. The family is neither dead nor dying. If Mark Twain could remark that the reports of his death had been greatly exaggerated, we might say the same thing about the family. It is changing, yes, but it is neither dead nor dying. And the family will persist because it serves persisting human needs.[1]

Pessimists among the social scientists have predicted the family's demise. True, the statistics and realities of family brokenness are grim, and no one of us has remained personally untouched in one way or another.

Furthermore, social science tells us that the family has lost important functions that once bound it together as a unit. Most family units are no longer necessary for economic production, nor are they the primary focus of education, nor a center of religious worship and instruction. With factories, public schools, social agencies, supermarkets, and religious institutions, who needs the family? And, one might add, with artificial insemination and *in vitro* fertilization, who needs the marriage bed to produce family members?

But there is one thing central to the family that no other institution offers: emotional and physical intimacy, nurture, and support. Those needs will never go out of style. They are absolutely vital for genuinely human life.

At the White House Conference on the Family earlier in this decade there was considerable heated debate. Anti-abortion and freedom-of-choice people clashed. Those pressing for more social supports for families in need did battle with those decrying government intervention. But about one thing there was firm agreement: the family is that basic primary group which best meets the needs for the nurture of human persons, for intimate commitment, for emotional and sexual fulfillment, indeed for the survival of what we know as human personality.

To say this is not to say that all is well in the home. To say this is not to say that what we usually call home is necessarily home at all. But to say this *is* to confess that each of us needs a place where the gifts of life make us more human, where we are linked with ongoing covenants to others, where we can return to lick our wounds, where we can take our shoes off, and where we know that—within the bounds of human capacity—we are loved simply because we *are*. Because that human need will not die, the need for the family will not die.

2. *The greater pluralism of family forms can be a good thing.* For the past several years my wife and I have lived in a central-city high rise in which there are 206 apartments. It is different from the small towns in which she and I grew up. It is different from suburbia, where our children grew up. On our floor are nine apartments. In none of these is there a traditional nuclear family. In fact, in only two of the nine are there married couples. But there are other families on our floor. They just do not fit the traditional mold.

Statistically, the nuclear family is clearly in the minority now in our country. It is one form among others. There are trial marriages. There are couples who have no intent of marrying. There are single-parent families. There are blended families as the result of previous marriages. There are gay families and lesbian families, usually without but sometimes with children. There are couples with children no longer home. There are couples who will remain permanently childless. There are families made up of an adult and an aging parent. There are families whose members share neither blood ties nor sexual relationships, yet they are constituted as families by enduring covenants. Pluralism of family forms is clearly the present reality.

In the midst of this change, however, there is enormous anxiety in many quarters, hence the appeal of the radical religious right on this issue. Nevertheless, Christian tradition does not endorse one correct form for family life. In fact, the church was rather slow in becoming concerned about the family as a unit. Not until the ninth century do records of distinctly Christian marriage liturgies appear, and the Roman Catholic Church did not insist upon Christian ceremonies until the late sixteenth century. And it was not until the nineteenth century that what we now term the nuclear family arose. Not until then did the extended family shrink to parents and their immediate offspring. Not until then was mothering seen as a full-time occupation. Not until then was childhood viewed as a separate era of life, with children to be shielded to protect their sexual, vocational, and moral innocence. Those who insist that there is only one Christian form for the family do not have Christian history on their side.

I believe that a greater pluralism of family forms *can* be a good thing, not that pluralism brings inevitable progress. Some marital and family experimentation has brought more pain and destruction than fulfillment and wholeness. But there is also evidence that some forms of marital behavior are improving, and that we are less tolerant of dehumanizing practices that were simply taken for granted in earlier days. In any event, when Jesus said that the sabbath is made for persons and not persons for the sabbath (Mark 2:27), he relativized every human institution. He taught us, in effect, that form follows function. If the function of marriage, family, and home is to serve authentic human needs, then forms should adapt to serve precisely that.

3. *Marriage is more a process than a state of being.* The song from *My Fair Lady* needs revision. "I'm getting married in the morning; ding, dong, the bells are going to chime" might better read "The bells will chime only when I know that I will never 'get married' once and for all but rather my partner and I will always be in the process of 'becoming married.'" Here is a helpful definition: mar-

riage is a moral relationship and process involving two persons who freely and in good faith commit themselves to live together, support each other, and grow in the capacity for caring throughout their mutual lifetime.[2]

Note some things about this definition. It emphasizes the freedom and good faith of each of the persons. It emphasizes their intention for a lifelong relationship. While usually one will be male and the other female, the definition does not exclude same-sex persons from authentic unions. The definition does not speak of caring simply for each other, but of caring beyond the marriage as well. The reality of the marriage, it suggests, does not depend on either church ceremony or legal status (however much we might value the importance of those); rather, the essential feature is the covenantal process between the persons.

Thus, marriage is not something that "happens to you." It is something that partners must do, and must keep doing, if it is to be real at all. As an ordained minister I have officiated at numerous wedding services, but I have never "married" anyone except Wilys Claire, and when we are at our best we know that we are in the process of becoming married. It is a never-ending process. The journey is our home.

But this is not a journey that two partners can make very well by themselves. Such a recognition is part of the symbolism and reality of the religious wedding service. There the community gathers around the couple, not only to celebrate but also to join in their process. If in an earlier day the extended family offered some emotional cushion and widened perspective for the couple, in the present day there is an intensity to the intimacy pattern that can at times become too heavy for the partners to bear. Possessiveness can creep in to complicate things further.

In recent mental-health literature the term "third place" has emerged. The claim is that there is a legitimate need for a third place, in addition to the intense involvements of family and job. Beyond the home and the work place, many of us need a third place of supportive caring and interaction. I have discovered this to be increasingly true for myself. Hence a cluster of special friends of both sexes with whom there is meaningful emotional intimacy has become important. I believe this intimacy is an expression of the New Testament's *koinonia*. These are companions with my spouse and with me in our journeying into marriage. I hope Wilys Claire does not have to carry more of my baggage on our trip than she ought.

4. Sexual fear is one of the family's greatest enemies. Male sexism, one basic expression of sexual fear, is a major threat to the family (even if the new religious right wing sees the matter quite differently, an issue to be explored further in chapter 9). We men have learned to fear and distrust our bodies. We have learned to put our reliance upon cognition, reason, power, and control. We have learned to distrust emotions, as well as the gender that has traditionally been said to be controlled by emotions. If there is any dominant internal cause for marital instability and discord and for family strife today, I strongly suspect that leading the list would be the pervasive ramifications of male sexism. To blame the women's movement is, sadly enough, one more example of our penchant for blaming the victim.

Another type of sexual fear is also an enemy of the family: the spirit-body dualism that is so much a part of our history. Because sexuality seems to be a body matter, it becomes inherently suspect, if not downright evil. Thus the double message with which many of us grew up: Sex is dirty—save it for someone you love.

The paradox is that out of this fear and denigration of the body comes an overemphasis on genital sexuality. In our society sexual activity becomes vested with such mystery and power that it is surrounded with taboos and mis-communications. Between parents and children a predictable dynamic occurs. Parents assume that children are nonsexual until puberty, and this assumption contributes to the silence about sexuality between parents and their children. The conspicuous silence gives children the message that sex is powerful, evil, and forbidden. Their desire to learn about this side of life is rejected, but their wish to know is heightened. They turn to sources of misinformation, and the gulf between child and parent widens.

Nevertheless, the conclusions of sexual researchers appear to be these.

- Humans are sexual beings from before birth to the end of their lives.
- As early as three years of age, children typically receive negative messages about their bodies; by this age most feel their genitals are a taboo area.
- Cross-culturally, children express the desire for more touching than they receive, and white Anglo-American children are among the least touched.
- Contrary to Freud, there is no latency stage of sexual disinterest; children between five and twelve are actively interested in sexual exploration and knowledge.
- The sexual knowledge desired by children is only secondarily concerned with reproduction; primarily they are interested in the feelings of pleasure they are experiencing and in the differences in body structures and feelings between males and females.
- Most parents, schools, and churches are doing a poor job of sexuality education; American children are particularly retarded in healthy sexual attitudes and information compared to many other cultures.
- Most sex-education materials written for children reflect a traditionally masculinist viewpoint (the

male is dominant, the female submissive, and in the sexual act the male is active, the female is passive).[3]

The resulting sexual fears are manifold: people who live as if their bodies were strangers; people who live with considerable sexual ignorance, fear, guilt, and dysfunction; people who succumb to a masculinist and hierarchical way of interpreting and responding to the world; people who yearn for a more whole life that seems to elude them.

Consider the ways in which family closeness is hindered by the fear of touch. I refer not to the misuse of physical touch in the family and its tragic results in incest victims, but to nongenital, nonexploitive, appropriate, warm-bodied human touching within the family, the kind that everyone needs to feel really loved and at home in the world. Edwin Brock's haunting poem paints the problem as he contrasts the experience of infancy and adulthood.

> You will not see the world at first:
> You will touch the flesh and you will cry.
> Years later you will cry because
> You see too much and touch too little.[4]

5. *Love is the central meaning of marriage and family.* Aldous Huxley has observed:

> Of all the worn, smudged, dog's-eared words in our vocabulary, "love" is surely the grubbiest, smelliest, slimiest. Bawled from a million pulpits, lasciviously crooned through hundreds of millions of loudspeakers, it has become an outrage to good taste and decent feeling, an obscenity which one hesitates to pronounce. And yet, it has to be pronounced, for, after all, Love is the last word.[5]

Huxley is right on both counts. "Love" is one of the

most abused, misused, and misunderstood words in our language. And it is the last word, the most fundamental of words about human experience.

What are we talking about? A meaningful relationship? That, too, is a much-abused term. Thus the *Playboy* cartoon depicts the couple waking up in bed, obviously a bit unsure of each other's identity as one says, "With whom am I having this meaningful relationship?" Surely it is something more than that.

Do we mean romantic love? Such love, surprisingly enough, was not commonly understood as even important to marriage for many centuries of the Christian era. It was nice if it happened, of course, but there was no sense that one should be in love with another in order to marry. The commitment to romantic love began to creep into our Western consciousness only around the thirteenth century. Yet we are of a double mind about romantic love and marriage. Much of our literature suggests that the song is wrong: love and marriage *don't* go together like a horse and carriage. Two of Western literature's greatest novels, Flaubert's *Madame Bovary* and Tolstoy's *Anna Karenina*, deal with the issue of love, but the protagonists are not in love with their husbands but rather with their "lovers." And the term lover takes on special significance since one's spouse is not usually thought of as one's lover.

Do people today marry for love? In the patchwork quilt of human emotions and motives there may be many reasons. Along with desire and attraction there may be the attempt to escape from parental authority, the fear of never marrying, the need to feel grown up in the eyes of others, revenge or rebounding from a broken relationship with another, the need for reassurance and self-esteem, the desire for respectability—to mention a few.

Nor is love to be confused with dependency, the "I can't get through life without you" feeling. That, as one psychologist rightly labels it, is more an addiction (with a dynamic similar to chemical dependency) than it is love.[6]

Rather, that love which is central to creative marriage and families is "a many-splendored thing." It is the desire for intimacy and the willingness to be vulnerable. It is rejoicing in the presence of the other. It is a commitment to the otherness of the other, a commitment to the other's uniqueness and growth, and an unwillingness to try to absorb or possess. Love is commitment to the wider causes of the other. It is friendship. And it rests upon a solid sense of the self's own worth and, ultimately, upon a deep sense of cosmic acceptance, of being at home in the universe.[7]

To be sure, if such love in its perfection were required to qualify one for marriage or family life, the Internal Revenue Service would never see a joint tax return. But my thesis is that the quest for such love makes the journeying creative. And *some* approximation of this love is necessary if there is to be a journey at all.

6. *The family is an agency for the transformation of the world.* The traditional wedding service contains this question: "Do you promise to keep yourself for him/her alone as long as you both shall live?" While the original intent of the question seems to refer to the exclusiveness of the sexual relationship, the words have often been taken to mean far more. The words have encouraged a "you and I alone" mentality wherein the couple gaze into each other's eyes and let the rest of the world go by. But such a mentality is good neither for marriage nor for the world.

The crisis in family relationships is not in the institution of marriage itself. It is much broader. The crisis is rooted in the alienation and depersonalizing life of modern society. And when marriages and families become romanticized and exclusive little islands, they cannot contribute to the larger solutions needed in the world. Furthermore, these little islands begin to sink under the enormous weight of the expectations for personal fulfillment that are brought to them.

Jesus' teaching on marriage and family itself has elements of paradox. Beyond question, he placed high value upon faithful marriage. Beyond a doubt, he cared deeply for his own immediate family, but he gave no hint that the immediate family ought to be one's primary concern or loyalty.

> While he was still speaking to the people, behold, his mother and his brothers stood outside, asking to speak to him. But he replied to the man who told him, "Who is my mother, and who are my brothers?" And stretching out his hand toward his disciples, he said, "Here are my mother and my brothers! For whoever does the will of my Father in heaven is my brother, and sister, and mother."
>
> —Matthew 12:46–50

While this may not be a popular sermon text for Mother's Day or Christian Family Sunday, it is there and it is important.

There are creative possibilities when the privatistic family is not idolized. Although many social scientists do not seem to recognize it, the family can be an effective agency in social change. It need not be simply a pawn in the hands of wider social and institutional forces. For example, families are major units of consumption. The power to decide what and how much to purchase need not be usurped by Madison Avenue advertising, as numerous alternative life-style families and consumer boycotts have effectively demonstrated. Furthermore, the family has considerable political relevance, for significant political socialization occurs in patterns of child-rearing. If Family X has highly authoritarian, rigid, and punitive relationships, and if Family Y has democratic and justice-oriented concerns built into its daily routine, those families are shaping different kinds of citizens.

Instead of being socially irrelevant, privatistic, and oriented only toward individual fulfillment, families have the potential to be open, hospitable, and socially concerned. Such families will not regard themselves as islands of intimacy in competition with the world for survival, but as small communities concerned with the redemption and renewal of the world.

7. *The grace of God is fundamental to all the above propositions.* This last thesis is not intended as a pious, sermonic ending. It must be said simply because it is profoundly true. Unless the ongoing, liberating, nurturing, affirming, life-giving presence of God continues to break into these small communities we call marriages and families, unless the Word continues to become flesh and dwell among us, none of the rest either makes sense or has hope. But because that does happen, there is, indeed, a future to celebrate. Human partnerships can be processes rather than static states of being. They can be relationships in which fidelity does not mean possessiveness. They can support a remarkable degree of intimacy and mutual vulnerability, and at the same time nurture and nourish the caring capacities for the wider world.

Sexual Politics and the Religious Right Wing: Some Theological Reflections

*T*he liberal religious press has not been remiss in the past several years in its critique of the "New Right" in religion and politics.[1] With its major criticisms I agree. In addition to sharp disagreement with the religious right on specific policy issues, the critics observe that these groups show such disturbing characteristics as these:

- a self-righteous claim to know and represent "true biblical morality"
- a vindictive and punitive attitude toward those with whom it disagrees
- a bias toward the white and the affluent in American society that ignores the socially, economically, sexually, and racially oppressed and the biblical-prophetic call for social justice
- a propensity to attack symptoms while its "solutions" ignore basic societal and world problems
- a desire to impose its own vision on a pluralistic society wherein many do not share the same assumptions or goals
- a militant commitment to a certain vision of the

American past in which the value system "was properly based on scriptural imperatives, patriotism, the traditional family, postponed gratification, discipline, moneymaking, preparing for war and, most important, moral rectitude."[2]

These criticisms are important ones. In addition, however, we need to press behind some of these judgments to attempt to understand the dynamics that appear to inform the thinking and actions of the religious right.

One description of that dynamic is simply "fear." Some years ago Richard Hofstadter insightfully analyzed the McCarthy era of the 1950s, calling it "the paranoid style in American politics."[3] For him, paranoia meant the feeling that there were forces threatening to undermine one's nation, society, way of life, and one's very existence, and that they must be stopped at all costs. Hofstadter's analysis has been resurrected recently for the light it sheds upon the current religious right.[4]

I find considerable truth in this thesis. People of the religious right do not actually seem to feel themselves in the moral majority, in spite of the name of their leading group. More characteristic is the sense of being the betrayed outsider. A *New York Times* analyst put it this way.

> They believe their moral and spiritual values are no longer reflected in public policy. In the past they were largely confident that the country was "Christian" and that government generally did act on their concern for such matters as family life and religion in the schools; they now say they feel like outsiders who must fight the forces of "secular humanism" and atheism.[5]

The Dualism of the Religious Right

Underlying this anxiety there is, I believe, a pervasive dualism in the world view of the religious right. A dualism splits into irreconcilable and opposing forces two realities which (while they may be distinguished) ultimately belong together. The dualism of the religious right has two interconnected manifestations, one political and the other sexual. The political manifestation emerges in claims such as these.

- The American nation is a chosen instrument of God, destined to lead the world to true faith and morals.
- Our prosperity is a result of Christian character, for righteousness exalts a nation.
- However, America is experiencing moral decay that threatens the nation and which, if not stopped, will give rise to dictatorships based on secular humanism.
- The world, thus, is divided into two opposing camps: America and its anticommunist allies pitted against godless communism.
- The proper role of divinely ordained government is the maintenance of a strong military establishment and the enforcement of basic laws, not regulation of the economy or interference in family affairs.
- True-believing Christians are called by God to be politically active and thus to restore America's virtue, its divine mission, and the proper role of its government.[6]

The dualistic tendencies are evident: good vs. evil, capitalism vs. communism, a government of law and defense vs. the welfare state, the chosen nation vs. those in darkness.

The sexual area is also a focus of considerable attention. Here the religious right opposes sex education in the public schools, abortion, homosexuality, pornography, the Equal Rights Amendment, women's and children's rights in general, family-planning programs, and various measures designed to assist broken families. The movement supports parental control of schools, the censorship of textbooks, and those programs that would support "the traditional family" and inculcate its values through public schools and civil law. The two familiar and ancient forms of sexual dualism are apparent: the hierarchical ordering of the sexes in patriarchal dualism and the spiritualistic denigration of the body in favor of the soul.

While the political and sexual dualisms appear quite different at the outset, I believe them to be closely related. But to probe that possibility, I must turn from the descriptive to a more critical analysis.

Political Dualism

The political dimensions of the religious right are illumined by Robert Bellah's classic interpretation of American "civil religion."[7] Borrowing the concept of civil religion from Rousseau, Bellah argued that every nation has some sort of religiosity which forms the glue holding that society together. It may draw upon a particular organized religion, but is never identical with it. This civil religion is expressed through national symbols, rituals, civil "holy" days, and public ceremonies. As such, it is neither good nor bad, neither creative nor destructive, though it may be either or both, depending upon the particular manifestation. It is simply the attempt to interpret the nation's experience in terms of that which transcends the nation. In the white American experience, early dominated by Puritan Protestants, there was a strong tendency to draw upon biblical categories such as the exodus (from the Old World), led by Moses (often identified as George Washington), into the new land that was to become the New Jerusalem. The theme of the Chosen People with a particular and vital mission on earth was crucial, and it merged into the notion of manifest destiny. American civil religion, in comparison to that in some other societies, was never anticlerical or militantly secular.

In some aspects, the religious right is as American as apple pie. It has, however, singled out the most conservative, militant, and nationalistic possibilities of our civil-religion heritage and has found precedents in the Bible for them.

Biblically, zealous nationalism emerged within a generation of the exodus and persisted for some centuries despite the contrary voices of the major prophets. After the exile there were at least two major groups in Judaism, and perhaps more. In one of them a genuinely dualistic conspiracy theory appeared, partly under the influence of Zoroastrianism. Here God was believed opposed by a demonic counterforce stirring up earthly opposition against the agents of righteousness. This apocalyptic dualism appears to have been the phenomenon of a dispossessed people unable to hold in tension their religious vision and the difficulties of their actual situation. For this section of Judaism, history had become a battleground between the armies of good and evil, a conspiracy theory receiving its articulation in the book of Daniel.[8]

A few centuries later in the apocalyptic book of Revelation the classic form of the conspiracy theory is set forth in ways reflected by today's religious right. Evil emanates from Satan, who breeds moral corruption and heresy. Yet God has ordained the final destruction of the evil forces and a total victory for the people of God who, if they are to rule, must be perfectly righteous and correct in their beliefs. Enemies are stereotyped as utterly lacking in redemptive possibilities, and hence their destruction in order that the source of evil might be eliminated is a logical conclusion.

Two related themes evident in today's religious right find biblical support. One is that of redemptive violence. Violence expressed through Yahweh directly or through

Yahweh's righteous people has the power to defeat evil and to bring peace. Whether one looks at the Song of Miriam (Exodus 15), or the flood story (especially Genesis 6:11–13), or certain of the psalms (see, for example, Psalm 58:10–11), or the destruction of Jericho under Joshua's leadership (Joshua 6:17–21), or numerous other Old Testament accounts, the theme is abundantly present.

The second (and related) theme is the connection between being right and being victorious. Here is one reading of the Deuteronomic philosophy of history: righteousness brings prosperity while wickedness brings ruin. The moral of this reading is evident: be good so as to be triumphant. While a deeper, more subtle reading of Deuteronomic history shows the viewpoint in that document to be much more complex, the simple interpretation above can easily be found there by those who wish to find it.[9]

Nor are these readings of the Bible foreign to certain elements of our American heritage. The Puritans took from the book of Revelation a dualistic world view and a conviction that violence would inaugurate God's kingdom. As Winthrop Hudson put it, "The New England story was viewed as a continuation of John Foxe's narrative of the pitched battles between Christ and Antichrist that had marked the course of human history from the beginning."[10] Leading Puritan preachers labored to build an invincible holy commonwealth, and when a large group emigrated to America from corrupt England, John Fiske described their zeal as "the desire to lead godly lives and to drive out sin from the community."[11]

The good-evil dualism, redemptive violence, and righteousness-equals-prosperity themes could be traced through numerous chapters of our religious and political past. They would be found in differing ways in John Adams and elements of the Revolutionary War; in the genocide against the Native Americans; in the Civil War with its "Battle Hymn of the Republic"; in nativist Protestantism with its anti-Mason and anti-Catholic movements; in the (sometimes violent) resistance to the Irish immigration; in the Spanish-American War; in Woodrow Wilson and John Foster Dulles; in the "Red Scare" of 1919–1920 and the McCarthyism of the 1950s; in certain zealots of the New Left in the 1960s—and again the religious right. The myth of the superhero carries on these themes in American popular culture: the Lone Ranger, Superman, Batman, Captain Marvel, or Captain America—the superhero with pure character and motivations, extraordinary powers, and the task of redeeming Eden from the forces of evil.

Thus there is nothing very new about the political dualism of the current religious right. But, as did its precedents, such dualism brings with it enormous theological and hence practical problems. Any political dualism subverts radical monotheism. If we believe that God alone is sovereign, then there can be no independent power of evil with whom God is locked in eternal battle. If we believe in the prophetic tradition of scripture, no human movement or position can be absolutized. The prophetic tradition reminds us that since human freedom is one of God's gifts, there is always the possibility of human change; no vindictive destruction by "the evil ones" can be countenanced. Furthermore, the prophetic tradition reminds us that sin is universal; there is no pure moral position, no total cure for social ills, and thus our best hopes come not in righteous crusades but in the steady confronting of ambiguous problems with a willingness to join what Bonhoeffer was fond of calling "the fellowship of dirty hands."

Sexual Dualism

The key word for the religious right's position on sexuality matters is *family*. Early in 1980 Senator Gordon

Humphrey of New Hampshire sent out a fund-raising letter. After criticizing President Carter's choices for advisors on the future of the American family, he wrote:

> For strong families are the foundation of strong America. For the American family is the most important moral force in America today. It is in the family that love, compassion and respect are taught. It is in the family that sexual morality and honor is taught. That's why the American Family Institute was founded. To fight for you and your family here in Washington. The American Family Institute was created to combat the anti-family propaganda of the militant homosexuals, radical women libbers and the sex lobby that for so long have been allowed free reign here in Washington.[12]

The religious right's generalized fear about sexuality—apparent in the manner in which it deals with such issues as sex education in the schools, pornography, and homosexuality—seems rooted in spiritualistic dualism. But the other side of the coin, sexist or patriarchal dualism, is more immediately evident. The omnibus Family Protection Act, introduced in several recent sessions by members of Congress sympathetic to the religious right on family issues, is particularly illuminating.[13] Among the bill's provisions is the denial of federal funds for sports activities that mix the sexes and for textbooks that promote the equality of women and men. The phrasing on the latter issue is this: ". . . if such materials would tend to denigrate, diminish or deny the role differences between the sexes as it has been historically understood in the United States." The bill would deny federal funding for sex education in the public schools, shelters for abused women and children, counseling concerning abortion procedures, divorce counseling, and advocacy of homosexual civil rights. Given positive support through favorable tax structures is the "traditional" nuclear family with the wife not working outside the home. As Rosemary Ruether comments, the bill gives a good picture of what its supporters mean by "family protection": "Its assumption is that if only women and children were reduced to their traditional dependency in the patriarchal family, made to pray regularly and shielded from disturbing new ideas, all would be well, and America would again become 'strong.' "[14]

There are significant connections between support for the traditional patriarchal family (which forms a "tough, manly character" for America) and policies of military superiority and international confrontations as tests of national virility. As Phyllis Schlafly put it during her campaign to defeat the Equal Rights Amendment: "Anyone who can't stand up to the women's libbers can't stand up to the Russians." Yet these connections between masculinism and militarism are not new to our social history.

Theodore Roosevelt is a key illustration. His Rough Riders won their acclaim in the Spanish-American War, a war not fought simply to remove Spain from the American sphere of influence or bring American progress to the heathen, but also a war clamored for by men needing a virility-challenging cause when the frontier was becoming obsolete and society was being tamed by the "new women." "It is this philosophy," comments social historian Joe Dubbert, "that lay behind Roosevelt's remark of 1895 that, after hearing the peace sentiment in America, he became convinced that what the country needed was a good war."[15] Later, when President Woodrow Wilson refused to confront Germany early in World War I, Roosevelt once again saw war as the supreme test of moral and physical manhood, saying, "Wilson has done more to emasculate American manhood and weaken its fiber than anyone else I can think of."[16] So also Lyndon Johnson and Richard Nixon both saw Vietnam as a test of America's manhood.

I emphasize this connection between masculinism and violence-prone politics because it is essential to understand that the political and sexual dualisms of the religious right are deeply intertwined. While this is more evident with the patriarchal form of sexual dualism, it is also true of its spiritualistic form. Consider the saved-damned dichotomy and its effects in violent politics. Once again the New England Puritans are revealing. Unlike the hierarchical Catholic society in which every person had a carefully graded place, the Puritan vision was a voluntaristic compact of equals. But it was also a community of the elect. Only the visible saints were eligible to vote, and the connection was close between the repression of nonconformists and the sharp distinction between the saved and the damned. When Calvinist predestination became modified by Arminianism, a much larger role for human effort in the salvation process was asserted. While exemplary conduct was still the visible sign of membership, this was now mated with hard work and economic achievement.

However, as Robert Bellah has noted in his analysis of this dynamic, certain groups—namely Native Americans and blacks—were excluded by definition: "There is first the assertion that a certain group of people lacks the qualities that would allow its members as individuals to rise, and then there is the systematic deprivation of that group of all the resources necessary for its members indeed to rise."[17] Thus, from its beginnings, white American society was based not only on the ideal of a community of voluntary participation but also on exclusion and repression— "first of all the intrapsychic repression of rejected impulse, and secondly the repression of those members of the society who represented those rejected impulses and had to be controlled and denied full membership."[18] While originally the distinction was put in religious terms (the elect vs. the reprobate), later it became moral (e.g., the economically successful vs. the failure).

At every stage of this development there was a strong tendency by those who believed themselves saved and good to forget their own evil and attribute it all to the reprobate. The rejection of the American black is particularly illustrative. Whites have commonly projected onto blacks impulses the whites found intolerable in themselves in terms of their own definitions of salvation and virtue, especially sexual desire, dirtiness, and sloth. Those bodily things that did not fit the image of the Protestant Ethic and that needed to be controlled in white Americans have thus been attributed to blacks, who are then punished. All this helps whites to keep their own self-control and be assured of their own goodness.[19] Thus the link between sexual spiritualism and exclusionary, violent politics becomes evident.

If America's racial minorities have functioned in one way in the inclusion-exclusion dynamic of white American identity, it may be that those who appear to deny God function in another way, the dynamic of sexist dualism. The "godless Communist" is the primary symbol. In current litanies of the religious right, the term "secular humanists" serves a similar function. Once again, part of the emotional dynamic at work is the struggle against inner impulses that threaten the integrity of the orthodox American self-image. In a highly masculinized sense of identity, one is supposed to be forever strong, self-reliant, and dependent upon no one else. But this masks the deep-seated dependency needs which are also part of us all. Such dependency needs, however, are uncomfortable for anyone who has invested a great deal in a personal identity of self-reliance (including anti-big government, unfettered free enterprise, and the like). To the extent that this is true, those who represent the extreme in antidependency—namely Communists and "secular humanists" who presumably deny the highest authority of all, God—will be the targets of unconscious resentment. They have apparently succeeded in making the break with all human dependency.

If both these dynamics are at work in that element of American identity that needs to be good and hence needs to project evil onto others, then it becomes painfully clear why, during our last and most barbaric war, the North Vietnamese and Viet Cong were treated so inhumanly. In their persons they brought together both targets of an anxious white American identity—they were nonwhite (hence, "gooks"), and as Communists they were identified as God-deniers.[20]

While I recognize some of the limitations inherent in such psychosocial analysis, I hope it will be taken with some seriousness. For if one is to speak in theologically constructive ways, one must respond not only to the more obvious issues voiced by the religious right but also to the dynamics of anxiety and fear in American identity, which the right's message is effectively tapping. A "cultural fundamentalism" in the right-wing reaction counts on the yearning of millions of Americans for a return to a simpler, more innocent time of unlimited American power and resources, a time of dependable authority and social conformity, a time when the sanctity and stability of the family seemed secure. Now, in the face of rootlessness, heterogeneity, and uncertain authority patterns, Americans crave a secure identity.[21] That this identity quest leads toward false securities through rejection of those who appear to embody our own insecurities is not simply a psychological problem. It is, fundamentally, a theological issue.

Some Theological Reflections

Is there a response from the heart of the Christian gospel to the new religious right? To those who so fear the body that they have an inordinate anxiety about all sexuality issues, there is the Word made flesh, God's stamp of approval upon the body as medium of divine love. To those who find threatening a society wherein sex roles are challenged and becoming more fluid, to those who find strength primarily in masculine force and physical power, there is One who strangely inverts our understandings of power and who invites us out of the bondage of patriarchy into the new human reality. To those whose insecurity is so painful that they must find scapegoats on whom to lay blame for all anxieties and evils, to those who must prove that they are more Christian and more American than others, there is that One who demonstrates the triumph of grace announcing that all are free to live as those who are accepted. To those for whom the future is so fearful that their trust is found in past solutions and in nostalgia for a small-town white middle America, there is the vision of a future wherein the meek of the earth will find their place and the full humanity of all will be affirmed.

These are visions of the gospel. There is much in mainstream Protestantism to affirm this. There is an irenic theological spirit that tries to listen carefully to all sides. So, in spite of the many distortions—indeed dangerous distortions—of the religious right, all Christians might find things to affirm. Together we can say that this nation will find its true destiny only in light of God's purposes. We can agree that the Bible is profoundly relevant to politics and that Christians have the obligation to exercise responsible citizenship. We have some important common ground.

From the mainstream Protestant dialectic between Calvinist and Lutheran roots, Christians can affirm some important correctives about the relations of church and state. The religious right believes that law should be used to enforce certain versions of morality rooted in specific religious traditions. In response to this, however, consider the dialectic posed by Lutheranism and Calvinism. Lutheranism, building on a two-kingdom theory, saw the state as "the order of creation" with only an ordering or preserving function, not a saving or humanizing function. The Calvinist position, by contrast, was that the state participated not only in God's ordering of the world but also in God's redeeming of the world. The state had a christological purpose. The Lutheran heritage asserted that the gospel had nothing directly to do with the law or politics or the governance of the world. The gospel, rather, was directed toward shaping the individual, who could then be a citizen with Christian motivations. The Calvinists contended that the gospel had direct implications for political programs in order that God's redemption might be manifest in public life as well as in private. The Lutheran tradition emphasized the future of God's reign beyond history, while the Calvinist emphasized God's renewing work in history as well.

Each of these traditions by itself is subject to distortion. Together they form a creative dialectic. The religious right, I fear, has embraced the weaknesses of both. From an exaggeration of the Lutheran side they perceive the state heavily in terms of law, order, and coercion. They see its function as primarily to provide order, defense, and restraint—not the positive contribution of humanizing life through social improvement. From one side of the Calvinist interpretation, the religious right emphasizes the theocratic possibility—the public rule of the "saints" and the political establishment of religious truth.

Christians need the creative tension of these Reformation traditions. We can affirm with our Calvinist forebears that God's central purposes for the state are not simply control but the positive humanization of life. With our Lutheran forebears we can affirm that, while the state must be God's servant, it is answerable only to God and not to the church. Thus, the state is free to be politically mature and not directly answerable to those believing themselves to be saints whose correct doctrine and morals confirm their positions of political authority. From both sides of the Reformation we can affirm that the sovereignty of God means that no human movement or position can claim final truth. We can acknowledge that those who wish to rule the commonwealth also have feet of clay.

Apart from an overly optimistic time earlier in this century when the theme of social transformation was deeply influenced by a doctrine of inevitable progress, the Christian heritage has not been utopian. We are not offered any illusion that the world can be made safe for our particular ideals, much less that another war will make things safe for peace. Because the vision is future oriented, we are not offered the hope that past solutions will bring us security or that nostalgia for an idealized vision of small-town white middle America will bring us righteousness.

What we are offered is a vision of transformation of all life, which is the liberation of all life. It is not the power of a moral majority but the vision of a remnant who can hear and identify with the meek of the earth, those everywhere dispossessed by white male privilege and power. It is not a vision that equates righteousness with prosperity, but one that finds God's righteousness impelling us toward solidarity with the world's oppressed. It is a vision that takes Christ's open-ended invitation seriously—"Come unto me, all ye that labour and are heavy laden, and I will give you rest [Matt.11:28, KJV]"—and refuses to amend it by adding "except, of course, for gays, people with leftist leanings, women who want to be ordained, and all social misfits who clearly belong somewhere else."[22]

Perhaps this vision at its root implies a transformation of our understanding of human nature itself.[23] The danger in any activist piety is precisely what the religious right so tragically exemplifies: the masculinist model of the authentic human as one who is forever in quest of mastery and success, charged by a stern, male God to carry out and enforce "his" commands. We are beginning to learn that under the dominance of this model we have had to repress too much of ourselves. We have learned to be terrified by those whose skin is different. And we have learned to resist any genuine cultural diversity because it threatens our definitions of the good and the right.

But there is a vision that knows the sovereign God not only as external and commanding but also as deeply inner and vulnerable, and as Cosmic Lover who lures us away from our false notions of security. It is a vision of the lordship of Christ, who as the Incarnate One gives us the security to be fully human and fully enfleshed so we can truly feel the joy and the pain of all embodied life. It is a vision of the transformation of all life which knows that American civil religion need not be the worship of the American nation, but an understanding of our cultural experience in light of the Universal One who beckons us toward the reality of one human family.

· 10 ·

Protestant Attitudes
Toward Abortion

Early Protestant attitudes toward abortion show considerable continuity with those of the pre-sixteenth-century church. The major Reformers—Martin Luther (1483–1546), Philip Melanchthon (1497–1560), and John Calvin (1509–1564)—were at least as conservative as their Roman Catholic counterparts on the issues of ensoulment and the gravity of abortion. Indeed, some historians believe that these Reformers indirectly but significantly contributed to the present papal position on the subject.[1]

The Reformers insisted upon the full humanity of the fetus from the time of conception. Their insistence arose, however, less from attention to the abortion issue itself than from their concern about the doctrines of original sin and predestination. Full humanity of the conceptus was believed necessary if the mind and spirit as well as the body of nascent life were to be involved in the consequences of the human fall.

Luther reclaimed the traducian position of the early Church Fathers in regard to ensoulment. This position held that the soul of the fetus along with its body was inherited from its parents. Influenced by the embryology of Aristotle and Galen, however, Luther assumed that the semen alone contained life and that the woman provided only nourishment for that life. Hence the father (through the power of God) was the source of the fetal soul. Melanchthon's theory of ensoulment was creationist, the belief that God directly creates the soul of each nascent life. Both of these Reformers, however, insisted upon the full humanity of the conceptus regardless of its gestational stage.

With Melanchthon, Calvin was creationist concerning ensoulment. With Luther, Calvin was concerned about the depth of human need and the radical nature of God's grace in the face of original sin. His particularly strong doctrine of predestination gave additional force to the contention that the fetus from its earliest stage was already *homo*, fully a person, for this life was believed to be primordially destined to be saved or damned.

The major Reformers, then, were rigorously opposed to abortion at any stage of pregnancy. Moreover, they had significantly enhanced the fetal status for reasons more basically doctrinal than for ethical reasons against abortion. Regarding fetal status, they were more conservative than the sixteenth-century Roman Catholic Church, which still maintained the Septuagint's distinction between the "unformed" and the "formed" fetus, and with it a consequent distinction in the gravity of abortion, depending on its timing. The Reformation's strong affirmations of justification by grace and forgiveness of sin, however, were to provide many later Protestants with theological perspectives and religious resources for dealing with abortion as a situation of ambiguity, compromise, and value conflict.

In seventeenth-century England, both Anglicans and Puritans continued to oppose abortion, but made the distinction between the unformed and the formed fetus. At the same time, the English Puritans initiated changes in the traditional understanding of marriage. Companionship was now seen as marriage's primary end, to which the ends of procreation and the restraint of lust were believed subordinate. This companionate view gradually became the dominant Protestant interpretation, and with it came the groundwork for justifiable abortions in cases of mortal conflict between woman and fetus. Indeed, by the late eighteenth century, English physicans were commonly urging and performing abortions to save threatened women.

Eighteenth and Nineteenth Centuries

American Protestantism manifested at least three major developments relevant to the abortion issue during the eighteenth and nineteenth centuries. One was a loss of interest in the human status of the fetus. Puritan predestinationists pressed Calvin's position on salvation, but with different results. Convinced that the individual's eternal destiny was fixed well before conception and gestation, the Puritans saw little to be gained from speculation about fetal ontology. Protestants generally lost touch with the earlier traditions on abortion and were inclined to appeal directly to scripture, where the early Jewish view and most subsequent texts supported full humanity only at birth. The pietist and revivalist groups of this period were disinclined to reflect about fetal humanity, for they were principally concerned with adult conversion. While they continued the typical Protestant opposition to abortion, their emphasis was often more restricted and practical: abortion was wrong because it was used, frequently at least, as a cover-up for sexual sins.

A strongly pro-fertility norm emerged in large segments of nineteenth-century American Protestantism, further buttressing antiabortion sentiments. Women must bear children if they were to be fulfilled as women. Furthermore, as God's New Israel, America had a crucial destiny in the world's salvation, and population growth was desirable to that end. Abortion thus was not simply an individual sin but also a social evil that denied society its needed citizens, economic producers, and defenders.

A significant countervailing influence on the abortion issue also emerged in nineteenth-century American Protestantism, however: the rise of social idealism and the Social Gospel movement. Those trends were less concerned about abortion than about the more visibly disadvantaged. But their particular concern for women's dignity, expressed in the suffrage movement, laid important foundations for later theories of both justifiable abortion and abortion on request.

Twentieth-century Influences

During the first half of the twentieth century, while official American Protestant opposition to abortion largely continued, the attitudes of numerous Protestant individuals were gradually being altered by several factors.[2] Under the impact of secularization, certainties that once had undergirded theological opposition to abortion became less certain. If to earlier Protestants the presence of each fetus in the womb was an expression of God's mysterious providence, to later Protestants the fetal presence was explained by natural processes, including human mistakes as well as human planning.

Furthermore, the mid-century abortion reform movement drew upon themes of great importance to the Protestant tradition itself, particularly human self-determination and the obligation to exercise rational control over nature. While the latter-day view of self-determination may have been a highly individualistic and secularized version of the Reformation's image of Christian liberty, it is nevertheless inexplicable apart from that historical connection.

A third factor was the waning vision of a Protestant

America. The failure of the Protestant-inspired prohibition law was a reminder that religious pluralism had replaced Protestant hegemony. America was no longer a society in which moral convictions that arose from particular Protestant theologies could be sanctioned by legislation. Thus, the distinction between a sin and a crime gained currency: what a particular religious group deemed sinful on its own doctrinal grounds ought not to be socially legislated as criminal without a much broader moral consensus on the issue. This distinction was further to erode Protestant support for antiabortion legislation.

Patterns in Contemporary Protestant Thought

In their theological reasoning, Protestants tend to take the church's tradition less seriously than they take the Bible. Those Protestants who look to scripture for specific moral instruction rather than for more general ethical principles, however, discover an absence of biblical texts specifically forbidding or permitting induced abortions. Indeed, the Old Testament does not typically view the fetus as fully human life. Exodus 21:22–25, for example, simply demands monetary compensation from the guilty party who causes a woman's miscarriage. Only if the woman herself dies does the charge become homicide, the offender being sentenced to death. Nevertheless, there are significant themes in both Old and New Testaments upon which Protestants typically draw for guidance in the abortion question. Life is a gift from God, and human reproduction is a process of sharing in God's creative powers (Psalm 139:13). Human beings are created not simply for comfort and pleasure but more basically for fulfillment, which often involves sacrifice for others (John 15:13). Life and death belong to God's providence, and there is no human right to extinguish life apart from persuasive evidence that such action expresses God's will in a tragic situation (Philippians 1:21–24). However general these biblical principles are, many Protestants insist that even they must be understood within the framework provided by the central ethical norm of scripture: the love commandment, which includes the dimensions of justice and mercy.

The major historical positions and influences mentioned earlier are present in the contemporary configurations of Protestant opinion on abortion. The perspectives range along a continuum from antiabortion to abortion on request, with perhaps the larger number of ethicists and Protestant groups affirming the justifiable-but-tragic abortion in certain situations of value conflict.

The antiabortion position is voiced by Dietrich Bonhoeffer, Paul Ramsey, Helmut Thielicke, and, with qualification, Karl Barth. Regarding the ensoulment issue, these ethicists maintain that it is not necessary to describe the fetus as a person. Rather, it is crucial that the fetus be recognized as a human individual; it is en route to becoming personal, but at all times it possesses the full sanctity of human life. Thus, two arguments are interwoven. First, biological data, especially at the stage of segmentation, establish human individuality. Second, Christian faith insists that the dignity of human life is not founded upon the individual's utility but rather is an alien dignity conferred by God and not admitting relative degrees of worth. While additional antiabortion arguments are typically added to the two above, the central issue is held to be the inviolable right to life of the fetus as a human individual, and not the weighing of competing values. Antiabortion Protestants, however, usually incorporate some version of the traditional Roman Catholic "principle of double effect" to argue that in certain extreme situations abortion is permitted because it is not the direct and willful taking of innocent life but rather the indirect result of saving life.

Abortion on request is more recent in the literature of Protestant ethics, although it has its articulate defenders. Proponents of this position argue that only wanted babies should be born. They typically maintain that permissive legal systems better protect women's lives and health, minimize social discrimination, and protect the autonomy of the medical profession. Here the principal concern is the woman's right to control over her own body and its reproductive processes, against those double standards that would permit others (usually males) to make choices on her behalf. As Joseph Fletcher observed some years ago, "Maybe an unexpressed and powerful objection is that responsible abortion, especially upon request, may give women the final control over reproduction."[3] The earlier Protestant emphases on self-determination, rational control of nature, equality, social justice, and the dignity of women enter strongly into this position. The real question, proponents argue, is not so much how we can justify abortion, but rather how we can justify compulsory childbearing.

The third general approach, sometimes called the justifiable abortion, lies somewhere between the first two, affirming arguments of each but differing from both. Rights of both fetus and woman are to be highly valued, but in theory and in practice neither ought to be absolutized. The elevation of one single right, it is argued, removes the inherent moral ambiguity of abortion decisions and oversimplifies other relevant moral factors. Instead of absolute rights, it is better to speak of competing rights and values. Together with the woman's right to self-determination and the value of human fetal life, a complex range of relational, social, medical, economic, and psychological values must be weighed, inasmuch as God cares for all these dimensions. Thus, each problem pregnancy has its own uniqueness, its own moral tragedy, and its possible alternatives. Christians must rely on God's grace and forgiveness as they make these ambiguous decisions.[4]

A Direction for the Future: A Pro-choice Theology in Feminist Perspective

Protestant feminists have charted new directions for the ethics of abortion in recent times by uncovering the misogyny embedded in the mainstream religious discussion of the issue.[5] They have argued that the "pro-life" position is more accurately described as "pro-fetus," and that the "pro-choice" position is actually "pro-woman." The former position has its origin in the ecclesiastical and sexual struggle over the control of procreative power: will men control it, or will women? For centuries the men have won in that struggle. But the pro-woman position finds its grounding in significantly different values. It is not a pro-abortion posture. It recognizes the moral ambiguity of every abortion decision. It clearly acknowledges that those who affirm procreative choice as an important moral good do not maintain that resorting to abortion is ever a desirable way of expressing such choice. They insist that the desirability of abortion's availability not be confused with the desirability of the act as such.

Certain critical assumptions in pro-choice theology differ from those common to the Christian tradition on the issue.[6] According to pro-woman arguments, life does not begin at the moment of fertilization or viability, but, morally speaking, with the woman's life prior to the conception. Moreover, the fetus's life cannot be considered simply as a separate entity detached from the woman, but must be viewed as a new dimension of life in addition to an already fully alive person. Furthermore, the decision to terminate a pregnancy must be seen as one that can express deep reverence for life, not only for the woman herself but also for the quality of potential life.

Feminist Protestant ethics are now uncovering distortions in the male-shaped historical record of the abortion discussion. Males have romanticized biological procreation as the central metaphor for divine blessing. Even so, there is overall in Christian history a relative disinterest in the question of abortion; it has not been a major ethical preoccupation. Protestant clergy did not rally in support of the proposed nineteenth-century antiabortion laws in the United States. Until the latter part of the last century, both natural-law tradition and Protestant biblical interpretations strongly tended to define abortion as the interruption of pregnancy *after* ensoulment, that is after quickening or feeling of fetal movement; thus early termination of pregnancy was not perceived as abortion. Finally, prior to the development of safe medical abortion procedures, one of the principal objections to abortion was the concern for the woman's health—an argument that now is voiced by the pro-choice side.

The core of the feminist argument is this: The moral status of the fetus simply does not deserve greater standing than does that of the pregnant woman. As Beverly Wildung Harrison says:

> The distinctly human power is not our biologic capacity to bear children, but our power actively to love, to nurture, to care for one another and to shape one another's existence in cultural and social interaction. To equate a biologic process with full normative humanity is crass biologic reductionism, and such reductionism is never practiced in religious ethics except when women's lives and well-being are involved.[7]

What, then, is a responsible Christian position, indeed an authentic pro-life position? Feminist Protestants maintain that such a position would genuinely enhance women's well-being and minimize the necessity for abortions. The necessity for abortions will be reduced only when the causes of problem pregnancy are directly addressed: contraceptive failure within marriage, the results of sexual violence, and the results of "coercive sexuality" (young males are typically taught that sexual prowess is the measure of their masculinity without responsibility for the consequences, and young females are taught that sexual appeal is the measure of their femininity, with total responsibility for the sexual consequences).[8]

Official Church Positions

A variety of public policy issues on abortion have concerned Protestant ethicists. Does a pro-choice public policy tend to cheapen or to enhance human dignity and the value of human life generally, and how can the evidence be assessed? Does a pro-choice public policy enhance racial equality or is it a disguised attack on racial minorities? What should be the relation of abortion policies to the population problem? What abortion policies best protect the freedoms of religion and conscience both of women with problem pregnancies and of medical personnel?

During the 1950s and 1960s several American Protestant denominations and ecumenical groups publicly affirmed positions on abortion. Since the 1973 U.S. Supreme Court rulings (*Roe* v. *Wade, Doe* v. *Bolton*), there have been additional Protestant policy statements. Most of these have acknowledged the moral ambiguity in abortion decisions. Most have recognized that the rights of both the fetus and the woman are important, and that neither should be absolutized. Most have acknowledged that the attempt to legislate a particular theological doctrine is a violation of religious liberty.

The statements have yet to go beyond the dilemma of

the particular abortion decision itself. The churches need to adopt a *genuinely* pro-life position, in the broadest, most inclusive sense of that term. Such a position will enhance women's well-being and minimize the necessity of abortions. It will support more medical research into reliable contraception for males as well as for females. It will insist on more adequate control of the production and distribution of contraception materials (some of which have been dangerously misleading and hence tragically destructive). It will support education for male responsibility in contraception, in procreation, and in long-term child care and nurture. It will support more widespread and effective sexuality education. It will challenge the destructive masculinist myths that women exist primarily to meet the sexual needs of men and that they are really fulfilled only through their procreative capacities.

Some Protestant denominations have remained officially silent on the abortion issue, encouraging their members to exercise prayerful freedom of conscience in such decisions. On the one hand, this seems to be a very appropriate respect for religious liberty. On the other hand, it is a retreat—a regrettable retreat—from engagement with the roots of the problem. When the churches fully face up to the thinly disguised oppression of women in the current abortion debate, a more genuine respect-for-life ethos may emerge.

· 11 ·

Spirit, Body, or Person?
Some Implications for
Medical Care

*T*here are a variety of ways in which the person as an ethical concept in medical care could be addressed.[1] For example, one could look at the venerable tradition of natural law to see how numerous principles and rules for medical care have been derived from certain understandings of what is natural to the constitution and destiny of the person. The Roman Catholic tradition has used this approach extensively.

Or one could consider the meanings of the word human and the word person as they are used as adjectives. Does human life always mean personal life? The distinction is important, as is obvious from the abortion and the death-and-dying debates in recent years. Is human life always personal life, and, if not, does less-than-personal life make the same moral claims as does a fully developed human person?

Closely related to this issue are the principles of the sanctity of life and the quality of life. Those who are committed most fundamentally to a sanctity-of-life principle usually argue that human life in whatever form and at whatever stage is to be accorded all the respect and protections due to any living person. Thus, fetal life from the moment of conception is to be considered fully human or personal life. Others, however, argue that the quality-of-life principle is fundamental. Difficult though it may be, distinctions must be made. This does not mean, they would argue, that people can become callous about non-personal or subpersonal biological human life. Human life should be highly respected in early fetal stages or in the permanently comatose stage, but our responsibilities to that life are morally different from when personhood is evident.

Still another approach might be an examination of the individual person and the social person. In making our medical decisions shall we consider most basically the rights of the individual and our duties toward that person, or shall we pay more attention to the consequences of our medical decisions for the widest social benefits for the larger community of persons? For example, what about the rights of a married couple who are carriers of a serious genetic disease? Should that couple be allowed to procreate even though society will have to bear the main burden for caring for a grossly deformed child?

Finally, one could look at the various roles that persons assume in the medical context. Who is the patient? What are the self-understandings of that patient in his or her illness? What are the appropriate roles of family members and friends? What effect do the various professional self-concepts of physicians, nurses, pastors, chaplains, social workers, and others have as they interact around the one who is ill?

Here then are five possible approaches to the concept of personhood in medicine. All of them are important. But I choose to take a somewhat different approach, simply because I believe that it, too, is of basic importance. Indeed, we who are members of the Christian church, which proclaims an incarnationalist faith, have a particular stake in this issue. The question is: Are persons spirits or bodies?

I assume that a person is neither a spirit nor a body but a unity. Human beings are "embodied spirits" or "spirited bodies." And this is not, I suggest, simply an interesting theological or philosophical problem but a fundamental issue of enormous practical importance in medical care and elsewhere.

First, a little historical excursion is necessary. Humans exist in history as fish exist in water, and we understand neither ourselves nor what we do day by day without understanding our roots.

The Christian religious heritage on this issue is rich, complex, and uneven. The Old Testament displays a remarkable sense of the unity of the person. The person is not treated as simply a soul temporarily inhabiting a body, nor is the person understood as fundamentally material. There is a wholeness about the biblical concept of selfhood. The Hebrews were accustomed to using various parts of the body as symbols for the whole. Thus the heart, the kidneys, the bowels, or other organs each could stand for a unitary self. There was no sharp distinction between health in all its dimensions and salvation. In fact, the root meanings of the words for salvation, healing, wholeness, and health all point to the same source.

Several centuries before Christ, however, in late Hellenistic Greece, a profound dualism of body and spirit arose. The spirit was considered eternal and the body temporal. The spirit was believed good and the body was believed to be suspect if not downright evil. Salvation meant escape from temporality and materiality and embodiment into the life of the eternal spirit.

While this spiritualistic dualism was foreign to the Old Testament, it did make its inroads into early Christianity. Traces of it can be found in the New Testament; it is abundantly present in the theologies of the early Church Fathers in the first few centuries. The result was a very mixed picture. In one sense salvation was spiritualized. Salvation seemed to have little if anything to do with the body. The body was denigrated. In another sense, it was the Christian church that spawned the hospital movement in the West. The church was the first institution to provide care for those in physical distress and even for those considered beyond the possibility of physical healing.

Nevertheless, it is probably fair to say that Christians took sides with the spirit and paid less attention to or even were deeply suspicious of the body. Thus, in the Middle Ages the church frequently resisted the advances of medical science and expressed horror over the practice of studying cadavers to learn more about bodily functions. Centuries later the church was unprepared for the "body thinkers" of the nineteenth century. Darwin, Freud, Marx—each of these giants of Western thought in his own way was a thinker of the body. But the church was unprepared for them. The church's continuing discomfort about human sexuality is still another indication of the ongoing power of the body-spirit split and the hold of spiritualistic dualism on Christian understanding.

The story of medicine in the West is somewhat different. But it did not escape its own body-spirit split. As medicine began to grow in scientific understanding and as a profession, it had to fight against theological rules and ecclesiastical taboos that shackled the searching mind. When, several centuries ago, medicine began to decline as an art and rise as a science, it found its philosophical foundation in René Descartes, the seventeenth-century French philosopher. To Descartes, the body was essentially an intricate machine. This concept was congenial to the developing scientific mind set of the age. And it led to an immense and growing knowledge of the biological nuts and bolts of the person. But in the process the person became understood as a fascinating machine in need of repairs when he or she was ill. And the results of this kind of dualism, now a *biologistic* dualism, have encouraged hospital staff people to talk about "the hernia in room 215" and "the appendectomy in 421." Jane Smith and John Jones lost something of their personal identities and became biological machines in need of repair.

Hand in hand with these tendencies, people came to think of the medical doctor as high priest of the body and the minister as high priest of the soul. While that is a neat division of labor, it still splits the patient in two in ways inimical to the healing process.

What about the physician as high priest of the body? In Western society the medical person was typically regarded as a religious functionary until a few hundred years ago. For most of history it was believed that diseases were either divinely or demonically caused. With the rise of modern science, medicine began to work its own wondrous cures on the body, and the physician soon shifted in the high-priestly role to the domain of the body rather than the domain of the body-spirit or the spirit-body.

While the priestly status of medical doctors in modern society is beginning to change, there is still considerable sympathy for placing them on pedestals. In the public opinion polls of most-admired professions, physicians still are very near the top. In occupational rewards, they are still the highest paid profession. The public often accords to them assumptions of expertise on wide ranges of subjects quite apart from medicine itself. The doctor's opinions on foreign policy and school bond issues are listened to more carefully than most others' simply because that person is a doctor.

The religious rituals of clinics and hospitals further cement the image of physician as high priest of the body. Priests wear robes and special costumes. The doctor still wears a costume of white, and white is the symbol of purity and holiness. It divides the holy from the diseased. Priests use mysterious cultic languages, and medical priests speak in mysterious technical languages. I find myself involved in a familiar religious ritual when I visit my physician. I confess my sin, I am assured of absolution, I receive the prescription of penitential acts to be performed. And if all this seems to be stretching it a bit, consider that we still believe the words of our clergy to be "counsel" and the words of our lawyers to be "advice," but the words of our doctors are "orders," which must be religiously followed.

Although more and more women are entering the medical profession, the profession is still highly male-dominated. And in the centuries of the spirit-body or mind-body split in Western civilization, men have largely identified themselves with spirit and mind, and they have identified women with body and emotions. Thus women represent the lower part of the person needing control by the higher. As a case in point, I was addressing a meeting of medical specialists some time ago. It was, quite predictably, an all-male group. In the course of my remarks I raised the question of the impact of male domination on the profession and the quality of medical care. The question itself apparently so incensed a distinguished physician that he rose from his seat in the middle of my presentation and asked whether I would like to have a hernia repaired by a woman surgeon who was in the midst of a menstrual period or undergoing menopause.

What about clergy, the high priests of the soul? This, too, is beginning to change in very exciting and constructive ways. Clergy are beginning to see themselves as ministers to whole persons. Nevertheless, the spirit-body dualism dies hard. Clergy often forget that Christianity began as a religion of healing that involved the total self. Clergy often remain willfully ignorant of body issues in health and illness. And clergy still frequently consider

172

themselves to be second-class professionals in the hospital context, quickly deferring to physicians who have the more important work to do. Most fundamentally, clergy, as do other Christians, too often forget that Christianity is a profoundly incarnationalist faith. The magnificent prologue to the Fourth Gospel reminds us that the Word became flesh and dwelt among us full of grace and truth. And that Gospel reminds us that the Word *still* becomes flesh and dwells among us. The startling reality here proclaimed is that the most decisive self-disclosure of God is not in otherworldly mystical experience or in thought and doctrine, but *in flesh*.

Lest we think this body-spirit split has largely been overcome, we need to remember that in many aspects of medical care persons are still treated either as bodies or as souls but not as whole persons. Our sexuality is a case in point. Sexuality has been largely neglected as a health-care issue. Perhaps this is because it so dramatically exemplifies the essential body-spirit unity of human beings. When I speak of sexuality, I am not simply referring to genital activity. Sexuality is a much richer dimension of selfhood. It includes the possibility of genital activity, but it is much more. It is our way of being in the world as male or as female persons. It is our attitudes about ourselves as body-selves. It is our capacity for sensuousness and our longing for intimacy. It is God's ingenious way of calling us into communion, physically and spiritually.

But consider the many ways in which sexuality is neglected in medical care. A nurse on the cancer unit comments, "We don't see much intimacy here between husbands and wives or members of the families. I wonder why." The male coronary patient is told only that he can resume sexual activity when he can climb two flights of stairs without undue stress. But that is all the advice he receives, because no one on his medical team feels comfortable in talking any further about his sexuality and its relationship to his heart condition. The gay male cannot find understanding medical counsel because his physician is so uncomfortable with homosexuality. The woman visiting her gynecologist feels detached from her body by the impersonal clinical language the doctor uses. The spinal-cord-injured young adult male, victim of an automobile or motorcycle accident in his early manhood, spends nine months in the hospital and rehabilitation centers before anyone on the medical team breaks the curtain of silence about the meaning of his injury for his sexual life. In nursing homes the needs of the elderly for physical touch often remain unmet. There are no double beds for couples, and if a patient is discovered masturbating it causes an institutional crisis. A hospital patient dying of cancer and subjected to distressing bodily disfigurement is acutely aware of the need for touch and intimacy, but finds little if any conversation about these things. A few years ago when my wife had a breast biopsy, I was sitting on the edge of her bed as she was coming out of the anesthetic, holding her in my arms. Two nurses walked down the hall, and, glancing into the room, one said to the other in a distressed voice, "Well, I wonder what's going on in there!"

Human sexuality is a fundamental dimension of humanness, God's gift of both the physiological and the psychological grounding of the capacity to love. But it still remains largely unintegrated into day-to-day health care, because of professional discomfort with the unity of the body-self.

In the face of all this, important challenges to the body-spirit split in medical care are beginning to be heard from a variety of directions.[2]

The challenges come from sick people. Sick persons seem to be crying out for a double diagnosis. They need the medical diagnosis of the organ in trouble. But they are also interested in how their health is related to the whole of their lives: how they sleep, recreate, work, exercise, pray, what they dream of, what their sexual and family lives are, what they hate, love, fear, and hope. For almost instinctively they know that all this is involved in their illness and in their health.

The challenges are coming from the growing discovery of our national ill health. In spite of the best research and crisis medicine in the world, American longevity statistics are not impressive. People are beginning to question why 5 to 7 billion Valium and Librium tablets and twenty thousand tons of aspirin are consumed each year in our society.

The challenges are coming from the growing field of psychosomatic medicine, where there is an increasing understanding of how chronic illness is related to stress, tension, and anxiety.

The challenge takes the form of a political critique, with increasing awareness of gross inequities in health-care distribution in this country. Americans are awakening to the fact that only 3 percent of the national health-care budget is devoted to preventive medicine and health education. It is dawning upon us that the enormous increases in medical costs, far outstripping the inflation of the dollar, are not closely related to better health.

The challenges come from a consumer critique. People are realizing that the right to significant decisions about their living and their dying ought not to be assumed by professionals. More and more women are questioning the paternalistic ways in which male physicians have treated them. More and more women are questioning the medications and procedures typically prescribed for them by male doctors.

The challenges come from a cross-cultural critique. We Americans are learning from other cultures that our basic ways of conceptualizing health and disease may not be the final word. It just could be that other and more "primitive" cultures can teach us a great deal about health and illness.

The challenges are coming from modern physics. Post-Einsteinian physics is calling into question the very scientific method on which biomedicine is currently based. The new physics is reminding us of the inherent subjectivity of all diagnostic judgments and of the ways individual perceptions shape the nature, course, and outcome of illness and health.

The challenges are coming from a growing ecological awareness. People are learning that they cannot be healthy in a polluted environment. They are beginning to realize that social and political stress is a major health-care issue.

Most fundamentally, the challenges are coming from religion. In spite of the fact that Christianity has too long been captive to body-spirit dualism, churches and their theologies are beginning to rediscover some implications of an incarnationalist faith for human wholeness.

How should Christians respond to these challenges? One possible way is to be defensive. After all, some will say, there is nothing basically wrong with our health-care model and its image of the person; only a few cranks and neurotics are making noise. But there are ways to respond more creatively.[3]

As Christians we can address ourselves simultaneously to the physical, mental, and spiritual aspects of persons in illness and in health. We can recognize the split that has stripped the mind of its capacity to experience the body, the split that has stripped the body of its own powerful wisdom. This might mean that we become as interested in meditation, in emotions, in diet, and in exercise as we are in EKG charts, because we are aware of what predisposes a person to coronary trouble.

We can view health as a positive state and not simply as the absence of disease. It has been estimated that up to 75 percent of patients coming to primary-care physicians have no obvious organic disease; they simply do not feel well. We can ask what needs to be changed in our understanding and in our medical-care processes to promote what the World Health Organization sees as health: "complete physical and mental well-being" in which there is a high level of vigor, joy, and creativity.

We can emphasize preventive health-care measures and the responsibility of each individual for his or her own health, convinced that persons are their own best sources of health care. This means that the job of professionals is to share rather than to withhold or mystify with their knowledge about health and disease. It means that the professional might become a resource rather than an authority.

We can give attention to the importance of sensuousness and sexuality as vital dimensions of a person's health. The early church knew that healing often comes with the laying on of hands. The early church knew the importance of physical touch. The Old Testament appreciated the fact that the body is meant to be a garden of delight. The comfort of clergy, doctors, and nurses with their own sexuality is of paramount importance in this process. I sometimes wonder what regular family massage two or three times a week would do for our physical and emotional health (as well as for family relationships).

Christians can view illness as an opportunity for discovery as well as a time of misfortune. We can see the connections between feeling overburdened in life and having painful back problems. We can see the connections between chronic genitourinary problems and sexual anxiety. We can use the trauma of heart attacks to reassess life-styles.

And we can pledge ourselves to help change those social conditions that perpetuate ill health, pledge ourselves to divert defense spending to feed the poor. Vitamin prescriptions simply do not do very much for those in genuine poverty or for those who subsist daily on junk food. All our sophisticated medical advances will not mean very much in the face of nuclear fallout.

Where does all this leave us? A more wholistic view of the person will perhaps one day lead to a fundamental, paradigmatic shift in the understanding of health care. In spite of the many remarkable curative advances of modern medicine, the biomedical model—dominated by disease rather than health—still remains solidly entrenched in medical practice and in the institutions and technology that support it. In such a model the assumption is that health problems are due principally to disease and that disease happens quite outside a person's control. Medical schools are predominantly schools devoted to the study of disease, not to the study of health.

Unless there is a basic change in this model of personhood and health, modern society will continue to multiply extraordinarily complex and costly medical technology for the conquering of disease in the privileged, and it will continue to neglect the positive meanings of health and of disease prevention for everyone. Doctors will continue to look upon the ill person as an isolated individual and not see the relational and life-style patterns that have contributed to the illness. Patients will continue to undergo unnecessary surgery and overmedication. The complex problems of law and ethics in medical treatment will continue to multiply.

The Christian faith has a great deal to contribute to a paradigmatic shift in medical care. The Bible relates health to personal wholeness and to an entire way of life. The Bible views a person not as a spirit temporarily residing in a body, nor as a complex physical machine that can be repaired at will by the skilled medical mechanic. The basis for this new understanding ought to be particularly evident to Christians convinced that ours is an incarnationalist faith. The Word still becomes flesh and dwells among us, full of grace and truth.

· 12 ·

Toward Incarnation

*B*ernard Pomerance's play *The Elephant Man* is set in late nineteenth-century England and is based on the life of a man named John Merrick.[1] From birth Merrick suffered a mysterious skin and bone disorder which, by the time of his adulthood, left him a monstrous, repulsive travesty of the human body. He finally died in a London hospital in 1890. His head and his right arm were horribly deformed. His useless right arm was the size of a leg and ended in a hand that looked like a fish's fin. Though his left hand and arm were normal, their effect was to make the rest of his body all the more grotesque. His lower limbs were grossly deformed like his right arm and hand.

As the play unfolds, a doctor rescues John Merrick from a circus sideshow, hoping to provide this pitiful man some semblance of human care, even if in a hospital room, in his final days. The doctor concocts a scheme. He asks a noted actress of the London stage, Mrs. Kendal, to visit Merrick. She is instructed to draw him into ordinary social conversation, and then as she is about to leave, she is to say to him (words he would never have heard before), "I am very pleased to have made your acquaintance, Mr. Merrick." The doctor knows that she, as an accomplished stage professional, will be able to carry out this assignment without disclosing her own feelings. She is, in conclusion, to give Merrick a parting handshake—but with her left hand reaching toward his left hand, the only touchable part of him. The doctor and Mrs. Kendal rehearse it all.

The scene unfolds. Mrs. Kendal makes her entrance and successfully hides her reaction upon seeing Merrick. She makes the light social conversation of the day in her charming, urbane, witty manner. She is a woman of the world, somewhat superficial, with little to prepare her for such an encounter apart from her skills in artistic deception.

But as the visit continues she comes gradually, perhaps unconsciously, to look directly at John Merrick. She still sees the grotesque body, but now she also begins to see the whole person. She recognizes the intelligence and wit of one who can joke even if his face cannot smile. She begins to see *him*.

The time comes for her to leave. She rises and delivers the rehearsed exit line, "I am very pleased to have made your acquaintance, Mr. Merrick." And with a very deliberate movement she extends her hand. But, instead of her left hand, it is her right. Although Merrick attempts to take it with his good left hand, she insists on clasping hands with him as she would any other person—her right hand to his right hand, the grossly deformed one.

We are moved by that kind of human encounter. In faith we simply say, "There is Christ." Incarnate grace is alive.

But as the play continues we begin to realize something else. In the friendship that develops between the two, it is not only she who embodies Christ to him but also—at least as significantly—he to her. For through their relationship her humanity is deepened.

No one can claim sexual wholeness. Human beings live with deformities caused by fear and guilt, by the ravages of spiritualistic and sexist dualism, by sexual abuse and homophobia, by the curtains of silence and shame lowered even in this supposedly enlightened time. We live lives that are more rehearsed, superficial, and steeped in the craft of the stage than we would care to admit. We bear the marks of both a Mr. Merrick and a Mrs. Kendal.

And Christians sense that these sexuality issues reach far beyond the private and interpersonal life. "We know that the whole creation has been groaning in travail together until now; and not only the creation, but we ourselves . . . groan inwardly as we wait for . . . the redemption of our bodies [Rom. 8:22–23]."

But one of the central paradoxes of the incarnation is that it occurs in unexpected places. So we meet and touch. There is personal presence. We know again the meaning of the Word becoming flesh. We discern afresh the resurrection of the body. And we are surprised by joy.

NOTES

PREFACE

1. D.H. Lawrence, *Complete Poems*, vol. 3 (London: Heinemann Publishing Co., 1939), p. 41.

CHAPTER 1: *Between Two Gardens: Reflections on Spirituality and Sexuality*

1. See Paul Ricoeur, "Wonder, Eroticism, and Enigma," in *Sexuality and Identity*, Hendrik M. Ruitenbeek, ed. (New York: Dell, 1970), pp. 13ff. Cf. Margaret A. Farley, "Sexual Ethics," in *Encyclopedia of Bioethics* (New York: Free Press of Glencoe, 1978), pp. 1585f.
2. See my *Embodiment: An Approach to Sexuality and Christian Theology* (Minneapolis: Augsburg, 1978), pp. 17f., for further discussion of these points.
3. For this interpretation of the two gardens I am indebted to the United Church of Christ's report, *Human Sexuality: A Preliminary Study* (New York: United Church Press, 1977), pp. 64ff., and especially to the work of Phyllis Trible and Ralph Weltge therein.
4. See Matthew Fox, ed., *Western Spirituality: Historical Roots, Ecumenical Routes* (Notre Dame, IN: Fides/Claretian, 1979), especially Fox's introduction.
5. Mary Aileen Schmiel, "The Finest Music in the World: Exploring Celtic Spiritual Legacies," in ibid., pp. 166f.
6. Nicolas Berdyaev, "Salvation and Creativity: Two Understandings of Christianity," in ibid., p. 116.
7. Matthew Fox, "Roots and Routes in Western Spiritual Consciousness," in ibid., p. 4.
8. See my *Embodiment*, pp. 31ff., for fuller discussion of these themes.
9. Charles Davis, *Body as Spirit: The Nature of Religious Feeling* (New York: Seabury Press, 1976), p. 126.
10. See Matthew Fox, *A Spirituality Named Compassion and the Healing of the Global Village, Humpty Dumpty and Us* (Minneapolis: Winston Press, 1979), especially chap. 2.

1. Nikos Kazantzakis, *Report to Greco*, trans. P.A. Bien (Oxford: Bruno Cassirer, 1965), p. 43.
2. Rainer Maria Rilke, *The Letters of Rainer Maria Rilke and Princess Marie von Thurn und Taxis-Hohenlohe*, trans. Nora Wydenbruck (London: Hogarth, 1958), pp. 144f.
3. William Temple, *Nature, Man, and God* (London: Macmillan, 1953), p. 478.
4. See Tom F. Driver, *Patterns of Grace* (San Francisco: Harper & Row, 1977), p. 4; Carl E. Braaten and LaVonne Braaten, *The Living Temple* (New York: Harper & Row, 1976), p. 2.
5. Norman O. Brown, *Love's Body* (New York: Vintage Books, 1966), p. 221.
6. See, for example, Margaret R. Miles, *Fullness of Life: Historical Foundations for a New Asceticism* (Philadelphia: Westminster Press, 1981), pp. 9f.
7. Ibid., p. 158.
8. Ibid., pp. 79ff.
9. Ibid., p. 114.
10. See Richard Zaner, "The Alternating Reed," in *Theology and Body*, John Y. Fenton, ed. (Philadelphia: Westminster Press, 1974), pp. 53ff.
11. Ibid., p. 64.
12. Ernest Becker, *The Denial of Death* (New York: Free Press of Glencoe, 1973).
13. See John Y. Fenton, "Bodily Theology," in Fenton, op. cit., pp. 127 ff.; and Arthur A. Vogel, *Body Theology* (New York: Harper & Row, 1973), chap. 1.
14. Thornton Wilder, *Our Town* (New York: Harper & Row, 1938, 1957), p. 100.
15. I am indebted to Vogel, op. cit., for the interpretation of bodily experience as relationality in this and the following paragraph.
16. Martin Buber, *I and Thou*, trans. Walter Kaufman (New York: Charles Scribner's Sons, 1970), p. 69.
17. I am indebted to Carter Heyward, "In the Beginning Is the Relation: Toward a Christian Ethic of Sexuality," *Integrity Forum* 7 (Lent 1981): 1ff., for her suggestive exposition of Buber and for the way she grounds the entire theological task relationally.
18. See ibid., p. 2.
19. George S. Hendry, "Christology," in *A Dictionary of Christian Theology*, Alan Richardson, ed. (Philadelphia: Westminster Press, 1969), p. 51.

20. See Tom F. Driver, *Christ in a Changing World* (New York: Crossroad, 1981). Driver has criticized me for implying a static Christology in my earlier writings on sexuality (see his pp. 52ff. and 133f.). The criticism is fair, for I did not give adequate attention to this important issue. I hope it is somewhat remedied in the present chapter. I have chosen not to attempt to develop the trinitarian implications in this essay, however. That is a task for another time, though I appreciate Driver's concern for this matter as well.

21. See Isabel Carter Heyward, *The Redemption of God* (Washington, DC: University Press of America, 1982), pp. 31ff.

22. See Rosemary Radford Ruether, *To Change the World: Christology and Cultural Criticism* (New York: Crossroad, 1981), chap. 3.

23. See ibid., chap. 4.

24. See Driver, op. cit., chap. 3, especially p. 44.

25. See ibid., p. 3. Driver uses Dorothee Sölle's term "christofascism" in this regard.

26. See Heyward, *The Redemption of God*, p. 197.

27. Norman Pittenger, *Christology Reconsidered* (London: S.C.M. Press, 1970), p. 40.

28. Heyward, ibid., p. 199.

29. See Donald M. Baille, *God Was in Christ* (New York: Harper & Row, 1948), pp. 116f.

30. H.A. Williams, *True Resurrection* (New York: Harper & Row, 1972), pp. 51f.

31. See Driver, op. cit., p. 60.

32. For a brief history of the Logos concept see Paul R. Helsel, "Logos," in *An Encyclopedia of Religion*, Vergilius Ferm, ed. (New York: Philosophical Library, Inc., 1945), pp. 449f.

33. John B. Cobb Jr., *Christ in a Pluralistic Age* (Philadelphia: Westminster Press, 1975), p. 71.

34. Bernard Lee, "The Appetite of God," in *Religious Experience and Process Theology*, Harry James Cargos and Bernard Lee, eds. (New York: Paulist Press, 1976), p. 369. I am indebted to Lee's observations about the connections between the human appetitive experience and God.

35. Ibid., p. 375.

36. Richard Rohr, "An Appetite for Wholeness," *Sojourners* 11 (November 1982): 30.

37. Bernard Lee cites Henry Nelson Wieman, *The Source of Human Good*, as being particularly suggestive in describing this phenomenon. See Lee, op. cit., pp. 378ff.

38. Quoted in ibid., p. 380.
39. See my *Embodiment: An Approach to Sexuality and Christian Theology* (Minneapolis: Augsburg, 1978), pp. 25ff., for a more extended discussion of sexuality and language.
40. An appropriate undergirding for this understanding of sexuality as language is a symbolic interactionist social theory. See ibid., pp. 27ff.
41. See André Guindon, *The Sexual Language* (Ottawa: University of Ottawa Press, 1977); James P. Hanigan, *What Are They Saying About Sexual Morality?* (Paramus, NJ: Paulist/Newman Press, 1982), pp. 85ff.
42. Quoted in Terry Eagleton, *The Body as Language* (London: Sheed & Ward, 1970), pp. 13f. Eagleton's entire treatment of Christ and language is suggestive. See especially chaps. 1 and 2.
43. See Elizabeth Dodson Gray, *Green Paradise Lost* (Wellesley, MA: Roundtable Press, 1979, 1981), pp. 58ff. Gray is here drawing upon the insights of Ronald J. Glasser, *The Body Is the Hero*.
44. Pierre Teilhard de Chardin, *Science and Christ* (New York: Harper & Row, 1968), pp. 12f. Cf. Lee, op. cit., pp. 382f.
45. For a more detailed discussion of pleasure see my *Embodiment*, pp. 87ff. and 265f.
46. See Matthew Fox, *A Spirituality Named Compassion* (Minneapolis: Winston Press, 1979), chap. 4, and *Whee! We, Wee All the Way Home* (Wilmington, NC: Consortium Books, 1976).
47. W.H. Auden, *Collected Poems*, ed. Edward Mendelson (New York: Random House, 1976), p. 308.

CHAPTER 3: *On Men's Liberation*

1. Allan Sillitoe, *The Loneliness of the Long-distance Runner* (New York: Signet/New American Library, 1959), pp. 37–38.
2. Valerie Saiving's article "The Human Situation: A Feminine View" was originally published in *The Journal of Religion* (April 1960), and has since been reprinted in *Womanspirit Rising*, Carol P. Christ and Judith Plaskow, eds. (San Francisco: Harper & Row, 1979).
3. Daniel C. Maguire has insightfully analyzed the effects of distorted masculinism on theology and ethics in his important article "The Feminization of God and Ethics," *Christianity and Crisis*, March 15, 1982.
4. I am indebted to Fasteau, op. cit., pp. 200f., for his description of this phenomenon.

5. One of the most useful discussions of this dynamic and others is by James R. Zullo, "Male Homophobia," in *Prejudice*, Timothy McCarthy, ed. (Romeoville, IL: Christian Brothers National Office, 1982).

CHAPTER 4: *Sexuality Issues in American Judaism and Roman Catholicism*

1. Useful sources on the Jewish situation include Allen B. Bennett, "Jewish Views of Sexuality," in *Religion and Sexuality: Judaic-Christian Viewpoints in the U.S.A.*, John M. Holland, ed. (San Francisco: Association of Sexologists, 1981); David M. Feldman, *Marital Relations, Birth Control, and Abortion in Jewish Law* (New York: Schocken Books, 1974); Robert Gordis, *Love and Sex: A Modern Jewish Perspective* (New York: Farrar, Straus, Giroux, 1978); and M.M. Kellner, ed., *Contemporary Jewish Ethics* (New York: Sanhedrin Press, 1978).

2. See Aviva Cantor, "A Jewish Woman's Haggadah"; Rita Gross, "Female God Language in a Jewish Context"; Naomi Janowitz and Maggie Wenig, "Sabbath Prayers for Women"; and Judith Plaskow, "Bringing a Daughter into the Covenant," in *Womanspirit Rising*, Carol P. Christ and Judith Plaskow, eds. (San Francisco: Harper & Row, 1979).

3. See James H. Schulte, "Roman Catholic Views of Sexuality," in Holland, op. cit., and James P. Hanigan, *What Are They Saying About Sexual Morality?* (Paramus, NJ: Paulist/Newman Press, 1982).

4. See Charles E. Curran, *Moral Theology: A Continuing Journey* (Notre Dame, IN: University of Notre Dame, 1982), and *Themes in Fundamental Moral Theology* (Notre Dame, IN: University of Notre Dame, 1977); also Philip S. Keene, *Sexual Morality: A Catholic Perspective* (Paramus, NJ: Paulist/Newman Press, 1977).

5. Anthony Kosnick et al., *Human Sexuality: New Directions in American Catholic Thought* (Paramus, NJ: Paulist/Newman Press, 1977).

6. See Hanigan, op. cit., pp. 80f.

7. See Sacred Congregation for the Doctrine of the Faith, *Declaration on Certain Questions Concerning Sexual Ethics* (Washington, DC: United States Catholic Conference, 1976).

8. See Rosemary Ruether, *New Woman, New Earth* (New York: Seabury Press, 1975); *To Change the World: Christology and Cultural Criticism* (New York: Crossroad, 1981); and *Disputed Questions: On*

Being a Christian (Nashville: Abingdon Press, 1982); also Elisabeth Fiorenza, "Feminist Spirituality, Christian Identity, and Catholic Vision," in Christ and Plaskow, op. cit.

9. See Mary Daly, *Gyn/ecology* (Boston: Beacon Press, 1978).

10. Charles E. Curran, for example, argues that the Roman Catholic Church should reexamine its official position and modify it to affirm that contraceptive technology, though subject to abuse, can be "a human good." See *Moral Theology: A Continuing Journey*, chap. 7.

CHAPTER 5: *Sexuality in Protestant Interpretations*

1. I have treated some of these issues in a different form in *Embodiment: An Approach to Sexuality and Christian Theology* (Minneapolis: Augsburg, 1978); "Toward a Theology of Human Sexuality" in *Religion and Sexuality: Judaic-Christian Viewpoints in the U.S.A.*, John M. Holland, ed. (San Francisco: Association of Sexologists, 1981); and "Faith, Ethics, and Sexuality," in *Human Sexuality: A Preliminary Study* (New York: United Church Press, 1977), chap. 3.

2. For useful interpretations of the Reformation on sexuality see William Graham Cole, *Sex in Christianity and Psychoanalysis* (New York: Oxford University Press, 1955), chap. 4; Derrick Sherwin Bailey, *Common Sense About Sexual Ethics: A Christian View* (New York: Macmillan, 1962), chap. 2; and Otto A. Piper, *The Christian Interpretation of Sex* (London: Nisbet & Co., 1942), chap. 2.

3. See Eleanor L. McLaughlin, "Male and Female in Christian Tradition: Was There a Reformation in the Sixteenth Century?" in *Male and Female: Christian Approaches to Sexuality*, Ruth Tiffany Barnhouse and Urban T. Holmes III, eds. (New York: Seabury Press, 1976).

4. Quoted in Bailey, op. cit., p. 57.

5. See Letha Scanzoni, "Protestant Views of Sexuality," in Holland, op. cit., pp. 32ff.

6. For a good overview of tendencies in recent Christian sexual ethics see Lisa Sowle Cahill, "Sexual Issues in Christian Theological Ethics," *Religious Studies Review* 4 (January 1978).

7. See Anthony M. Kosnick et al., *Human Sexuality: New Directions in American Catholic Thought* (Paramus, NJ: Paulist/Newman Press, 1977), pp. 92ff., and chapter 4 of the present book.

8. On this issue Norman Pittenger provides a good corrective to the

view of Helmut Thielicke. See Pittenger, *Making Sexuality Human* (New York: The Pilgrim Press, 1970), and Thielicke, *The Ethics of Sex*, trans. John V. Doberstein (New York: Harper & Row, 1964).

9. On this issue, D.S. Bailey provides a good corrective to the view of Karl Barth. See Bailey, op. cit., and Barth, *Church Dogmatics*, vol. 3, no. 4 (Edinburgh: T & T Clark, 1960).

10. I find Bailey's interpretation of divorce particularly helpful (op. cit., pp. 155ff.).

11. For a history of contraception see John T. Noonan, "Contraception," in *Encyclopedia of Bioethics*, vol. 1, Warren T. Reich, ed. (New York: Free Press of Glencoe, 1978), pp. 204ff.

12. On the varied treatments of homosexuality, see John Boswell, *Christianity, Social Tolerance, and Homosexuality* (Chicago: University of Chicago Press, 1980); Edward Batchelor Jr., ed., *Homosexuality and Ethics* (New York: The Pilgrim Press, 1980); and John J. McNeill, *The Church and the Homosexual* (Kansas City: Sheed Andrews and McMeel, 1976).

CHAPTER 7: *Religious and Moral Issues in Working with Homosexual Counselees*

1. See Robert Nugent, "Gay Ministry," *Ministries*, November 1980.

2. See Don S. Browning, *The Moral Context of Pastoral Care* (Philadelphia: Westminster Press, 1976).

3. See my *Embodiment: An Approach to Sexuality and Christian Theology* (Minneapolis: Augsburg, 1978), chap. 8.

4. See John Boswell, *Christianity, Social Tolerance, and Homosexuality* (Chicago: University of Chicago Press, 1980).

5. Gregory Baum, "Catholic Homosexuals," *Commonweal*, February 14, 1974, pp. 480f.

6. See Donald Goergen, *The Sexual Celibate* (New York: Seabury Press, 1975), and Janie Gustafson, *Celibate Passion* (San Francisco: Harper & Row, 1978).

7. See John Boswell, "A Crucial Juncture," *Integrity Forum* 6, no. 6 (1980).

CHAPTER 8: *The Family: Some Theses for Discussion*

1. Regarding this and certain other sociological judgments, I am indebted to conversations with my colleague Wilson Yates, and acknowledge with gratitude the influence of his important

forthcoming book on the family. See also his "The Family: A New Pluralism and a New Wholeness," *Theological Markings*, Spring 1982.
2. See Beverly Wildung Harrison, "Some Problems for Normative Christian Family Ethics," *Selected Papers, The American Society of Christian Ethics, 1977*, Thomas Ogletree, ed. (Dallas: American Society of Christian Ethics, 1977), p. 74.
3. See *SIECUS Report* 8 (November 1979): 6, and 8 (May–July 1980): 15.
4. Quoted in Conrad Bonafazi, *A Theology of Things* (Philadelphia: Lippincott, 1967), p. 54.
5. Aldous Huxley, *Tomorrow and Tomorrow and Tomorrow* (New York: Harper & Row, 1956), p. 68.
6. See Stanton Peele, *Love and Addiction* (New York: New American Library, 1975).
7. See H. Richard Niebuhr, *The Purpose of the Church and Its Ministry* (New York: Harper & Row, 1956), p. 35, for a splendid description of love.

CHAPTER 9: *Sexual Politics and
the Religious Right Wing:
Some Theological Reflections*

1. See, for example, "What's Wrong with Born-Again Politics? (A Symposium)," *Christian Century*, October 22, 1980; Ralph Clark Chandler, "Worshiping a Past That Never Was," and J. Mark Thomas, "Worshiping a Place That Isn't God," *Christianity and Crisis*, February 15, 1982.
2. Chandler, op. cit., p. 20.
3. See Richard Hofstadter, *The Paranoid Style in American Politics and Other Essays* (New York: Knopf, 1965).
4. See, for example, James Wall, editorial, *Christian Century*, October 22, 1980, pp. 995f; also Thomas J. McIntyre, *The Fear Brokers* (New York: The Pilgrim Press, 1979).
5. Kenneth A. Briggs, "Evangelicals Turning to Politics," *New York Times*, August 19, 1980.
6. See Robert Zwier and Richard Smith, "Christian Politics and the New Right," *Christian Century*, October 8, 1980, pp. 937ff.
7. See Robert Bellah, "Civil Religion in America," *Daedalus* 96, no. 1 (Winter 1967).
8. See Robert Jewett, *The Captain America Complex: The Dilemma of Zealous Nationalism* (Philadelphia: Westminster Press, 1973), especially pp. 116f. Though Jewett may overemphasize the

nationalistic phenomenon as dominating Judaism during this period, his point deserves attention. Balancing views which point out that this was characteristic of one important strain of Judaism may be found in Otto Ploger, *Theocracy and Eschatology*, trans. S. Rudman (Richmond, VA: John Knox Press, 1968), and in Paul Hanson, *The Dawn of Apocalyptic* (Philadelphia: Fortress Press, 1979).

9. I am indebted to my colleague Arthur L. Merrill for helpful counsel on aspects of Old Testament interpretation.

10. Quoted in Jewett, op. cit., p. 27.

11. See Robert Jewett and John Shelton Lawrence, *The American Monomyth* (Garden City, NY: Anchor/Doubleday, 1977), especially pp. 195f.

12. Solicitation letter from Senator Gordon Humphrey (no date).

13. See Rosemary Ruether, "Politics and the Family: Recapturing a Lost Issue," *Christianity and Crisis*, September 29, 1980, p. 262.

14. Ibid.

15. Joe L. Dubbert, *A Man's Place* (Englewood Cliffs, NJ: Prentice-Hall, 1979), p. 76.

16. Ibid., p. 192.

17. Robert Bellah, "Evil and the American Ethos," lecture sponsored by The Wright Institute at Grace Cathedral, San Francisco, February 22, 1970, p. 3.

18. Ibid., p. 5.

19. For further discussion of these phenomena in white racism see my *Embodiment: An Approach to Sexuality and Christian Theology* (Minneapolis: Augsburg, 1978), pp. 266ff.

20. I am again indebted to Robert Bellah for the suggestive analysis reflected in these two paragraphs.

21. See McIntyre, op. cit., especially pp. 11f., 41, 161.

22. Robert McAfee Brown, *Theology in a New Key* (Philadelphia: Westminster Press, 1978), p. 167.

23. Robert Bellah expresses this vision well in "Evil and the American Ethos."

CHAPTER 10: *Protestant Attitudes Toward Abortion*

1. See, for example, George Huntston Williams, "Religious Residues and Presuppositions in the American Debate on Abortion," *Theological Studies* 31 (1970): 13, 41.

2. See Ralph B. Potter Jr., "The Abortion Debate," in *Updating Life and Death: Essays in Ethics and Medicine*, Donald R. Cutler, ed. (Bos-

ton: Beacon Press, 1968), pp. 88f.; and Wilson Yates, *Family Planning on a Crowded Planet* (Minneapolis: Augsburg, 1971), pp. 63–78.

3. Joseph F. Fletcher, "A Protestant Minister's View," in *Abortion in a Changing World*, vol. 1, Robert E. Hall, ed. (New York: Columbia University Press, 1970), p. 27.

4. See James M. Gustafson, "A Protestant Ethical Approach," in *The Morality of Abortion: Legal and Historical Perspectives*, John Thomas Noonan, ed. (Cambridge: Harvard University Press, 1970).

5. See Beverly Wildung Harrison, "Theology of Pro-Choice: A Feminist Perspective," in *Abortion: The Moral Issues*, Edward Batchelor Jr., ed. (New York: The Pilgrim Press, 1982); and Joy M.K. Bussert, "Woman or Fetus: A Call for Compassion," monograph published by the Minnesota Council of Churches, 1982. While there are a number of feminist theologians writing on the abortion issue at this time, I particularly want to acknowledge my debt to Professor Harrison for both personal conversation and printed word, and I want to celebrate the significance of her new book on this issue: *Our Right to Choose* (Boston: Beacon Press, 1983).

6. See Bussert, op. cit., p. 3.

7. Harrison, op. cit., p. 220.

8. See Bussert, op. cit., p. 4.

CHAPTER 11: *Spirit, Body, or Person?*
Some Implications for Medical Care

1. I have previously elaborated a number of the themes in this chapter in *Human Medicine* (Minneapolis: Augsburg, 1973); *Rediscovering the Person in Medical Care* (Minneapolis: Augsburg, 1976); and *Embodiment: An Approach to Sexuality and Christian Theology* (Minneapolis: Augsburg, 1978).

2. For a helpful discussion of the challenges of wholistic medicine, see James S. Gordon, "The Paradigm of Holistic Medicine," in *Health for the Whole Person*, Arthur C. Hastings et al., eds. (Boulder, CO: Westview Press, 1980).

3. Additional suggestions concerning the new paradigm are elaborated in James F. Jekel, "A Biblical Basis for Whole-Person Health Care: Theoretical and Practical Models in Health and Healing," in *Whole-Person Medicine: An International Symposium*,

David E. Allen et al., eds. (Downers Grove, IL: InterVarsity Press, 1980).

CHAPTER 12: *Toward Incarnation*

1. See Bernard Pomerance, *The Elephant Man* (New York: Grove Press, 1979).